I & II Samuel

God Tests
a Nation
and Its Leaders

I & II Samuel

God Tests a Nation and Its Leaders

George S. Jr. and Charlotte U. Syme

ACCENT
Bible Curriculum

ADULT STUDENT
Bible Study Guide

This Bible Study Guide is part of an adult
curriculum designed to assist you in making
the entire Bible your Guide for daily living.

George S. Jr., and
Charlotte U. Syme/Authors
Judy Stonecipher/Managing Editor
James T. Dyet/Executive Editor
Robert L. Mosier/Publisher

Accent Bible Curriculum
Accent Publications, Inc.
12100 W. Sixth Avenue
P.O. Box 15337
Denver, Colorado 80215

CONTENTS

INTRODUCTION

The books of Samuel ought to be required reading for all who wield authority. Not only should presidents and governors be included, but also heads of schools, pastors of churches, fathers of families. There will scarcely be a Christian who does not in some manner have a responsibility of governing others for which God holds him answerable.

From one viewpoint, these books of Samuel may be studied as a treatise on accountability. At its beginning, God says to Eli—one of the chief men of his era—"them that honour me I will honour, and they that despise me shall be lightly esteemed" (I Samuel 2:30). Turning to the end of the books, we learn that the God of Israel said to David, "He that ruleth over men must be just, ruling in the fear of God" (II Samuel 23:3). All that lies between is an illustration of these two fiats. Keep in mind that the two books were originally written as one and were later divided for convenience in handling the scrolls.

Samuel may also be perceived as a study in contrasts between man's ideal man and God's ideal man, or between the natural man and the spiritual man. Saul and David are excellent examples for such a study.

Best of all, you can see Jesus in I and II Samuel. Through the experiences of David's life we see the life, ministry, work and future reign of our Lord. "Search the Scriptures," Jesus said, because "they are they which testify of me" (John 5:39). Learning of Him should be a goal of all Bible study.

As you study these lessons, you will want to familiarize yourself with the parallel passages in I Chronicles. They frequently bring out additional details of interest. You will also want to spend much time in the psalms of David, particularly those referred to as being related to the various lessons. David did not write his wonderful poetry in some ivory tower. They were wrought out of the crucible of his own many-faceted life and are his response to the sorrows and joys, the defeats and victories, the sins and restorations, that made up its fabric. This is why they speak so perfectly to countless thousands of others who face similar situations which sooner or later reach us all. We cannot truly understand the psalms apart from the life of the one who wrote them, nor can we really understand the man and his life apart from what his psalms reveal of him.

If you own or can borrow an English translation of the *Septuagint*, you will discover that it too adds interesting twists and details not found in our traditional text. The *Septuagint* is the version of the Old Testament translated from the Hebrew into Greek about 200 B.C. It is often abbreviated as LXX.

A rather untaught Christian who was accustomed to doing most of his Bible reading in the New Testament, accepted his teacher's challenge to read the book of First Samuel through at a sitting in order to get the total picture. The next week he came to Sunday School excited and offered this testimony: "People say the Old Testament is dull, but that Samuel is sure some reading—and lots to learn in it. We will be getting things we never knew before."

May you, too, approach this portion of God's Word with anticipation. And may you say when you have concluded it that you have seen the Lord and received instruction in righteousness that has brought your life closer to that which glorifies Him.

". . . the Lord seeth not as man seeth; for man looketh on the outward appearance, but the Lord looketh on the heart."

—I Samuel 16:7b

GOD MEETS A NATION'S NEEDS

I Samuel 1—3

Learn by Heart:
"I will raise me up a faithful priest, that shall do according to that which is in mine heart and in my mind: and I will build him a sure house; and he shall walk before mine anointed for ever" (I Samuel 2:35).

EVERY DAY WITH THE WORD

Monday	Godly child-training	Deuteronomy 6:1-15
Tuesday	A prayer and a vow	I Samuel 1:1-18
Wednesday	Sacrificial gratitude	I Samuel 1:19—2:11
Thursday	Two kinds of sons	I Samuel 2:12-26
Friday	Fathers are responsible	I Samuel 2:27-36
Saturday	A responsive son	I Samuel 3
Sunday	Children—God's heritage	Psalm 113; 127

Daniel 4:25; 5:21

I Samuel 2:6,7

Luke 1:52

How significant it is that the story of the Hebrew monarchy should begin with a description of an aching heart. Our God is the Lord of history. He "rules in the kingdom of men, and giveth it to whomsoever he will." It is He who kills and makes alive, who makes the rich and the poor. He puts down the mighty from their seats and exalts them of low degree. Yet He is not so busy with "mighty works of empire" that He overlooks the needs and heartaches of individuals.

One lonely mother needed a son to cradle in her arms, and a whole nation needed a prophetic spokesman to lead them back to the arms of their God. One tender miracle from the heart of an omnipotent Father supplied both.

A YIELDED MOTHER
(I Samuel 1:9-18; 2:12-17,22-36)

There is a growing attitude in our culture that having children is a curse on our society, and that parents of large families are to be condemned. It is one indication of how far we are drifting from the value systems of the Word of God. It was not so with the ancient Hebrews. They recognized fruitfulness as a mark of God's blessing. The parents of large families were congratulated and honored as those whom the Lord had deigned to favor.

Hannah's barren condition, then, was more than a personal disappointment; she and her contemporaries would interpret it as a judgment from God, or at least an evidence of His marked disfavor. Worse yet, since Elkanah had children by another wife, the disgrace was Hannah's alone to bear. Her contented husband, for all his protestations of devotion, was uncomprehending of the grief that tore her heart and the bitterness spawned by the taunts of the other woman who shared her home and husband.

Hannah knew the one place to take such grief. On a visit to the tabernacle at Shiloh, she poured it into the ears of the One who "maketh the barren woman...to be a joyful mother of children." In her desperation, she made a bold vow: if God would grant her a son, she would not keep the treasure for herself, but give him back to God (I Samuel 1:11).

Even here in the holy sanctuary, Hannah at first met only misunderstanding. Such laying hold on God must have been a rare sight at Shiloh. Eli, the aged high priest and God's official

The books of Samuel (they were originally one) introduce two great institutions of Israel: the monarchy and the prophetic order. Both revolve about Samuel.

Psalm 113:9

See the law of the Nazarite in Numbers 6:1-8.

representative in Israel, did not fail to take it all in. He decided she must be drunk (1:13,14). What a telling commentary on the low state to which Israel had fallen. We must presume that drunkenness was not uncommon in the house of God when the priests practiced open immorality.

Even in such a society, true godliness was not extinct. A Hannah could still rear a child to honor and serve the Lord. He has never left Himself without a witness. It is where Satan seems most completely in control that the faithful shine the brightest.

Hannah's faith was a triumphant one. Having cast her burden upon the Lord, she went home without it. She really believed God was going to answer her prayer. She had become bitter in her grief, had refused to eat, and spent her time complaining and crying. Now the bitterness was gone, the inner burden was eased, and the change showed in her renewed appetite and brightened expression. This is how it ought to be. If we have been in fellowship with the Lord and have left our burden with Him, people should be able to recognize the fact.

The God who gives life has a right to control it. Yet how often parents fail to acknowledge this. At the close of a Sunday evening service, a teenager presented himself in dedication for whatever service the Lord might ask. After brooding on it for half a week, the father stood up in prayer meeting with this testimony: "God knows He is welcome to anything I have except my son. I've great plans for that boy and have begun training him to take over my business. I will not give him up." Within four years he was dead and the business sold. His son became a minister.

It could not have been easy for Hannah to relinquish her little boy into the care of a half-blind old man who had failed as a parent (2:22-25), and to return home expecting to ease the ache of once more empty arms with only sweet memories, a praying heart, and busy hands that would sew little coats. But the God who wants the very best we have, always pays abundant interest on what is put into His hands. Hannah had five more babies (2:21).

It seems to be a way of God to begin the preparation of His servants with their parents. A godly home and early training in the Word of God is the most fertile soil in which to grow saints. Psychologists tell us that a child's basic personality and character traits are set by the age of three, and a Jesuit leader once said, "Give me a child for the first seven years and I care not who trains him thereafter."

Hannah probably had about three years with her son; yet Samuel from his earliest years reflected her piety and yieldedness. The Scripture describes his development, as it does that of our great High Priest of whom Samuel was only a type. It records the fact that Samuel grew "in favour both with the Lord, and also with men" (I Samuel 2:26).

There is evidence that a child might not be weaned until about three.

Compare Luke 2:52.

A RESPONSIVE SON
(I Samuel 3:1-10,18-21)

It is customary in many of our churches for Christian parents to publicly dedicate their babies to God, acknowledging thereby that they are a gift from Him, a trust and responsibility over which He still has primary rights. In this attitude we have the Scriptural example of Hannah.

Strictly speaking, however, such an act, if a church chooses to practice it, is not so much a dedication of our children as it is of ourselves, a commitment to rear them in His truth and by His standards, as prospective saints and servants of God. Inevitably, however, there comes a time when He will begin to speak to them directly, dealing with them less and less through us. Wise parents will resist the temptation to stand between their children and the voice of God.

We are not told how old Samuel was when such a time came for him. The artists make him look about seven. He might have been twelve or thirteen—certainly no more. The story of God's call to him and of his prompt and obedient response is familiar to every Primary child in the Sunday School. We often overlook the lessons to be learned from Eli's role in the incident.

The historian, Josephus, says he was 12. He may preserve an ancient tradition, or he may have been making a reasonable guess.

Eli must share with Hannah some of the credit for Samuel's responsiveness. He had been such a failure with his own sons that the judgment of God was already hanging over his head (I Samuel 2:27-36). Yet God had graciously given him another chance by making him guardian of the child destined to become His spokesman to the nation. And Eli showed that he was not the slave of his former mistakes.

What comfort this should be to anyone who grieves over having failed the Lord or fears he may have lost forever the privilege of service. Can you think of some other Scripture examples where the Lord proved Himself to be the God of "the second chance"?

When he knew that the Lord was calling Samuel, he might have offered to take the message for him or with him, perhaps pleading his greater experience with the Word of God. Instead, he taught Samuel how to respond and then declined to interfere.

He did later demand to know the message. This was in keeping with his responsibility as Samuel's

15

teacher. Anyone can claim a message or vision from God. Such claims must be checked against God's known Word to see whether it is in harmony or contradiction. If more people were careful to do this, false teachers would make far less headway in the church. Samuel's revelation coincided with that which an already recognized prophet of God had given Eli (I Samuel 2:27).

Cultists often make such claims. This is the way to guard against being taken in by them.

Finally, although it must have hurt to hear his judgment confirmed at the mouth of his young pupil, Eli did not become angry. Neither did he seek to justify himself or to deny that it was God who spoke. Men still find these methods handy substitutes for confession of sin and repentance. But Eli, with humility and submission, acknowledged the justice of God and the rightness of His sentence.

Eli's line was cut off as prophesied, but the Lord has immortalized him in His Word as an encouragement for all those who fear their failures have made them unfit for any usefulness.

The final fulfillment occurs in I Kings 2:26,27.

A woman who had gained a wide reputation as a teacher of women's home Bible classes was heartsick when her minister son deserted his wife and two children to elope with his secretary. "I can never teach again," she mourned, "for I must have failed as a mother."

To such a parent and to all who recognize their failures in handling their God-given responsibilities, the dealings of Eli with Samuel may serve as a comfort and a reminder that we can learn from our failures and be alert to redeem every new opportunity He offers to those who are willing and repentant and ready to grow by their mistakes.

The Lord, of course, holds an adult son responsible for his own behavior, just as He did the sons of Eli.

At the same time, we should not leave the lessons to be learned from the child Samuel himself to the Primary department of Sunday School. Through His completed Word, God still speaks to those who belong to Him. He speaks also to those who are not His—often through the voice of the preacher or another Christian—with the loving invitation to receive His Son.

Like Samuel, we too have an obligation to be alert to His call. If we do not know the source of the Word that speaks to us, we are responsible to investigate it in the same spirit that sent Samuel running to Eli. Many are guilty of failure in this matter when they reject the Bible as God's Word, calling it a man-made book filled with human errors. Thus they justify their refusal to heed its message.

Like Samuel, too, we must be quick to obey God and those whom He has placed. Perhaps our Lord was thinking in part of Samuel's example of listening and obeying when He admonished His disciples that they, too, must become as little children.

Samuel lived up to his early promise. He did not become puffed up or arrogant about any supposed spiritual superiority over Eli, but remained submissive and obedient. He continued to grow in the Lord and in the respect of the people. In due time, not only Eli, but the entire nation, knew that God in His goodness had sent a prophet among them (I Samuel 3:19-21).

DISCUSS IT AT HOME

• God held Eli responsible for his sons' evil. Can godly parents be permissive? Why is it an evidence of selfishness rather than love?

• How can we know when the Lord is dealing with our child? How may we ascertain when our stepping aside is getting out of God's way, and when it is failing our responsibility as the child's guide?

FOOD FOR THOUGHT

"Great trials seem to be necessary preparation for great duties."—Thompson

NOW TEST YOUR KNOWLEDGE

Who said it? Match these questions and answers (answers may be reused):

1. Am not I better to thee than ten sons?

2. O Lord of hosts, if thou wilt indeed look upon the affliction of thine handmaid. . .

3. How long wilt thou be drunken?

4. Do what seemeth thee good.

5. For this child I prayed.

6. My heart rejoiceth in the Lord, mine horn is exalted in the Lord.

7. Nay; but thou shalt give it me now: and if not, I will take it by force.

8. If a man sin against the Lord, who shall intreat for him?

9. The Lord saith, . . . them that honour me I will honour, and they that despise me shall be lightly esteemed.

10. Speak; for thy servant heareth.

11. His sons made themselves vile, and he restrained them not.

12. What is the thing that the Lord hath said unto thee?

a) a man of God   d) Elkanah   g) Peninnah

b) Eli   e) God   h) Samuel

c) Eli's son   f) Hannah

JEHOVAH VINDICATES HIS HOLINESS
I Samuel 4—7

EVERY DAY WITH THE WORD

Monday	Plan of the Ark	Exodus 25:1-22
Tuesday	Blessing or cursing	Deuteronomy 28:1-10, 15-25
Wednesday	Israel judged	I Samuel 4:1-11
Thursday	House of Eli judged	I Samuel 4:12-22
Friday	Philistines judged	I Samuel 5
Saturday	God's holiness defended	I Samuel 6
Sunday	Repentance and victory	I Samuel 7

"I simply cannot believe anymore," a distraught woman wrote a columnist. "I had so much faith in my prayers, and yet my son died. I don't understand it."

This poor mother was not aware of it, but she had a problem of misplaced faith. She had put her confidence in the sincerity or intensity or frequency of her prayers rather than in the God who is sovereign over the affairs of men and knew what was best for her and her son.

To insist that God must fulfill our wishes because of any action of our own, is not faith; it is a form of magic or superstition. This is true not merely of witch doctors' rituals; it can also be true of such worthy activities as prayer, fasting, and offerings. If we think they force God to do our bidding, we are on a level with Aladdin using his magic lamp. This was one of Israel's mistakes.

GOD DEFENDS HIS HONOR
(I Samuel 4:1-11; 5; 6:1-9,19-21)

While chapter four begins with the statement that "Israel went out against the Philistines to battle," the engagement was probably initiated by the expanding and invading Philistines. The Philistines' objective apparently was to subject the hill country of central Palestine and thus secure their control of the valley of Armageddon. They were already in possession of the central plain, which soon came to be called the plain of the Philistines. Archaeology has turned up evidence that shows they controlled the city of Beth-Shan which commanded the passage from the valley to the Jordan and the Sea of Galilee. The Philistines, therefore, put themselves in an array at Aphed on the road from the plain to Shiloh.

The two armies met at a place later named Ebenezer (I Samuel 7:12). This conflict is therefore known as the first battle of Ebenezer. It was apparently an indecisive one, although Israel suffered severe losses—four thousand men. The elders of Israel asked themselves, "Wherefore hath Jehovah smitten us to day?" (4:3). Although they correctly recognized their defeat came from the Lord, they should have remembered the Lord had promised victory to those who would "hearken diligently" to His voice.

The Ark of the Covenant was the visible symbol of Jehovah's presence with His people. It had been made to support the mercy seat between the cherubim where the Lord promised to commune with Israel. When the glory of the Lord came

The Philistines were a powerful seafaring people of Greek background who had pushed out from their Aegean homeland seeking new places to settle. They had established a strong foothold on the eastern shore of the Mediterranean, maintaining five strong city-states (Joshua 13:3) on the southwestern coastal plain of Canaan. The tenacity of their settlement is indicated by the fact that they gave their name, Palestine, as a permanent inheritance to the country.

upon the tabernacle, the mercy seat was, no doubt, established as God's meeting place with His people. As they went on their way to the Promised Land, the Ark and the cloud of the Lord went before them. Before the Ark, Jordan parted and Jericho's walls fell.

When Israel entered into their Promised Land, the Ark contained three objects: the stone tablets of the Law which reminded them that God had priority in their lives and was sovereign over their conduct; Aaron's rod that budded when his right to the high priesthood was questioned, a reminder that God was sovereign over their leadership and government; and a pot of manna, because God was their sustainer and supplier of all their needs. It was upon the mercy seat on the Ark that the high priest sprinkled the blood of the sin offering on the Day of Atonement (Yom Kippur) that the people might obtain mercy rather than judgment for their sins (Leviticus 16:14).

Exodus 16:33; Hebrews 9:4

Everything about the Ark was symbolic of Jesus Christ through whom we obtain mercy, become submissive to the Word and rule of God, and in whose name God supplies all our needs.

When Israel sought to force a victory over the Philistines by carrying the Ark into battle, they were committing an act of blasphemy. They were treating the Ark as if it were a heathen idol. The Lord had told them how to be assured of victory over their enemies, and Moses had recorded it (Deuteronomy 28:1,2). After they entered the Promised Land, Joshua called a solemn assembly of the people and read to them the blessings promised for obedience to God's law, and the curses that would accompany disobedience.

Joshua 8:30-35

Victory and security in their homeland were rewards of obedience to God's law; shame and defeat would be their lot if they forsook Jehovah and His standards.

Deuteronomy 28:15,25,37

I Samuel 2:12-17

Now Israel was backslidden; even their priests were men of the grossest appetites and passions. They had lost their high view of God's holiness and sovereignty, and were behaving with as much superstition as their pagan neighbors. They treated the Ark as if it were their god and would secure victory if it went to battle with them.

The Philistines were no less superstitious. They, too, thought the Ark was Israel's god. They had heard how He manifested His great power among the Egyptians (I Samuel 4:8), and the sight of the Ark filled them with terror. Instead of paralyzing them, however, it galvanized them to desperate action, and they won a great victory. The overconfident men of Israel fled in disarray (4:10). Triumphantly, the Philistines carried the Ark home and placed it in the temple of Dagon, their chief god. It appeared that the living God of Israel had been put to shame before a heathen idol.

This was a common practice among the ancients. The gods of defeated peoples were often brought to the god who defeated them to do him honor and service. Likewise Samson was humiliated in the temple of Dagon, and performed his last exploit there (Judges 16:23-30). The remains of King Saul were treated in like manner (I Samuel 31:1-10; I Chronicles 10:8-10).

The prophecy spoken through Samuel was fulfilled when Eli fell dead from the shock of hearing of the fourfold tragedy: Israel had fled! There was a great slaughter! His two sons had perished! And, crowning all, "the Ark of God is taken!" This was the blow that killed him (4:17,18).

The news was equally devastating to Eli's daughter-in-law, who promptly went into labor and was delivered of a son, but could comprehend nothing but "the glory is departed from Israel" (4:19-22).

Israel was humiliated in defeat, but not Jehovah. He is never honored by the success of a backsliding and blasphemous people, even if they invoke His name. He can defend His own glory; it was not long before the Philistines were far more eager to be rid of the Ark than they had been to capture it. Their own lifeless idol prostrated itself, and they were incapacitated by a humiliating sickness. In an effort to be rid of its baneful effects, they sent it from one Philistine city to another (I Samuel 5). Finally, in solemn conclave, they decided to return it to Israel (6:1-9).

Even the poor cattle, forced to carry the burden, were unhappy with it. Driven by a compulsion they did not understand, they deliberately walked away from their needy calves, lowing their protests with every step. Only when they reached Israelite territory and a spot suitable for sacrifice did they stop (6:10-14).

Although Israel greeted the Ark with rejoicing and sacrifices, they too soon regretted its presence among them. Because they handled it irreverently as an object of idle curiosity, it became as much a curse to them as it had been to the Philistines. But instead of seeking the reason for God's displeasure, they followed the Philistine example of banishing the Ark to another town. There it rested in obscurity for twenty years (6:13—7:2).

> "Men retain God in their written creed but depose him from the throne of their life."—Joseph Parker

Such is always the pattern when men choose to live their own way instead of repenting of their sins and seeking God's way. They do not want Him or any reminder of Him in their midst. Therefore they banish Him to an obscure corner of their lives, being content to let some professional "caretaker" make whatever gestures of attention seem necessary.

23

HE HONORS REPENTANCE
(I Samuel 7)

There is no record of Israel having sought Samuel's advice after the Philistines returned the Ark to them. At that time they still preferred to deal with the things of God according to their own way. It took twenty years for them to become fed up with the barrenness of their own sinful lives and the joylessness that went with being deprived of the opportunity to worship and serve God. They had long recognized that Samuel was God's spokesman to them, but for so long they failed to heed him.

I Samuel 3:20

When they were ready to seek the Lord, Samuel faithfully pointed out that true repentance required the putting away of sin. This meant destroying all their false idols and returning to the spirit and practice of the first commandment: "Thou shalt have no other gods before me." After doing this, they came together in a great service of worship and reconsecration (7:3-6).

Are there idols that take the place God demands for Himself in your life?

The Philistines saw in this great religious ceremony a perfect opportunity to enforce their power over Israel. What they succeeded in doing was demonstrating the power of those who are in right relationship with the Lord of hosts. When they were a fully equipped army of backslidden sinners, Israel had been ignominiously defeated. Now, as unarmed worshipers who had repented of their sins and drawn near to their God, they were invincible. The Lord Himself intervened for Israel, and they won a mighty victory (7:7-12).

In this incident we see how Samuel's judgeship differs from the previous ones. He was not called to lead the armies in a great military victory as his

DISCUSS IT AT HOME

• Are we guilty of allowing some of our Christian practices and methods of worship to degenerate into superstition?

• Think of some ways in which we are and are not justified in putting God to the test concerning any matter. Are we justified in seeking His will—by prayer or by a test—in any matter concerning which the Scriptures speak clearly? Why might the Philistines be permitted to test God in ways that would be condemned if Israel used them?

predecessors had been. God had personally stepped in with His weapons to rout the Philistines, and Samuel called on the nation to acknowledge and remember it. He was the last of the judges—after him, military and governmental functions would pass into the hands of kings.

Samuel is also recognized as the first of the prophets—those men of purely spiritual qualifications and responsibilities who would become the voice of God to both king and commoner, reminding them of their obligations to the One who is sovereign over all the affairs of both nations and individuals. Even after the advent of Saul, Samuel continued as the acknowledged spiritual leader of Israel, judging their temporal affairs, accepting their sacrifices and presenting them before the Lord, and speaking the words of the Lord to the people.

One of his primary prophetic functions to the nation appears to have been to lead them back to a remembrance and acknowledgment of the absolute holiness of Jehovah. It was to manifest His holiness to the world that Israel had been called out of Egypt; and they needed frequently to be reminded of it. Jehovah was not like the false gods of the heathen. A holy God is not to be manipulated or forced to do man's bidding by rites of magic or superstition; no visible representation is to be substituted for Him, so that His people become guilty of worshiping an idol; nor is His holiness to be profaned by irreverent treatment of anything that pertains to Him. It is with hearts, not rituals, that He is concerned. When the hearts of His people are right, they are invincible.

NOW TEST YOUR KNOWLEDGE

Choose the best answer:

1. Insisting that God must do man's bidding if he uses the correct rituals or other human means is a) magic; b) prayer; c) profanity.

2. Handling what pertains to God (His Word, name, worship, ordinances, etc.) in a way other than He has prescribed is a) magic; b) prayer; c) profanity.

3. Submitting ourselves and our problems to the Lord, seeking His will and glory in their solution is a) magic; b) prayer; c) profanity.

4. When we seek to use Him for our own ends and show irreverence to what pertains to Him we are failing to recognize His a) goodness; b) holiness; c) love.

5. The right path to God's blessing is a) repentance; b) more desperate prayer; c) more elaborate promises.

6. Hannah's prayer was answered because she a) prayed in the tabernacle; b) sought God's glory; c) was sincere.

7. Taking the Ark to war did not bring victory because it was a) not carried by Eli; b) not blessed by Samuel; c) being used as an object of superstition.

8. Victory came when Israel a) returned the Ark to Shiloh; b) forsook their sins; c) attacked Dagon.

FOOD FOR THOUGHT

"Religion and morality are the indispensable supports of political prosperity . . . Reason and experience both forbid us to expect that national morality can prevail in exclusion of religious principle."

—G. Washington

THE NATION REJECTS JEHOVAH
I Samuel 8; 12

Learn by Heart:
"Only fear the Lord, and serve him in truth with all your heart: for consider how great things he hath done for you" (I Samuel 12:24).

EVERY DAY WITH THE WORD

Monday	A king's concerns	Deuteronomy 17:14-20
Tuesday	Opting for conformity	I Samuel 8
Wednesday	Saul introduced	I Samuel 9
Thursday	A king chosen	I Samuel 10
Friday	Put to the test	I Samuel 11
Saturday	A faithful God	I Samuel 12
Sunday	Christian duty	Romans 13

A former chief usher, writing of his experiences while serving under nine presidents, had this to say about the atmosphere of the White House during the administration of Benjamin Harrison.

"Immediately after breakfast all the family would retire to the upper floor and be closeted in one of the rooms for a half hour of prayer. The entire atmosphere of the household was surcharged with religious feeling during this time. Until this ceremony had been completed, one could not go about one's daily duties without a feeling that prayer was being disturbed."

Ike Hoover, Forty-Two Years in the White House, p. 8.

Of basic importance to a people's well-being is not primarily whether their rulers are elected, appointed, or born to their positions, but whether they recognize they have a trust from God and a responsibility to carry out the principles of His Word. Were more rulers to follow the example of

President Harrison, how differently history might read.

A FAITHLESS PEOPLE
(I Samuel 8)

It is the Lord's ideal that those who accept the responsibility of leadership should look on themselves as shepherds, even servants. Foreseeing the day when Israel would demand a king, He had incorporated into the law the most important qualifications to be sought in a ruler. The king was not to be power-hungry (building a cavalry), pleasure-bent (amassing a harem), or materialistic (seeking wealth). Instead, he should spend a portion of every day making his own copy of God's Word, then studying it and practicing it.

Deuteronomy 17:14-20

In all his dealings with Israel, Samuel had admirably fulfilled this ideal of a shepherd-ruler. Yet even he, godly man that he was, was not exempt from the special temptations that come with power. He succumbed to two common weaknesses.

First, he sought to perpetuate his power and position in his sons. Already they had debased the moral tone of his leadership by using their offices as opportunities for personal gain (8:3). According to the law of Moses, those who exercised the office of priest were adequately provided for out of the tithes and sacrifices of the people.

"Grace is not hereditary," is Joseph Parker's comment on the activities of Samuel's two sons.

Only a covetous desire for personal enrichment beyond what God had ordained for them can explain the behavior of Samuel's sons. We have an obligation to support adequately those who

Leviticus 6:26-29; 7:6-10; 23:17-20; Numbers 18:8-18; 31:25-47; Deuteronomy 14:28,29; 18:3-8; 26:12.

represent and serve us—both politically and spiritually; we also have a right to expect that they in turn will base their decisions and actions on what is to our best interest rather than to their greatest enrichment.

Secondly, Samuel took it as a personal insult that a change of leadership should be as much as considered. In a special sense, of course, Samuel was God's choice of leadership for Israel. It is true, nevertheless, that all in authority hold their position from the Lord, for "the powers that be are ordained of God" (Romans 13:1), and, "The most High ruleth in the kingdom of men, and giveth it to whomsoever he will" (Daniel 4:32). Therefore, when one's person, or principles, or policies, are repudiated, a servant-leader will rise above personal hurt and accept the change as from the Lord. The change of leadership is either God's program, or—as in Samuel's case—the Lord is permitting people to experience the results of their own self-will.

Samuel took his hurt to the Lord and had his outlook straightened out (8:6-8). He was also given a description of the dangers of putting vast power into sinful human hands. Before acceding to the people's request, Samuel was to relay this description to them (8:9-18).

How well history has borne out this description of the behavior of rulers! The trappings of power hold insatiable fascination, not only for the man on top, but even for the minor functionaries who operate at the fringes of their bureaucracies. The ability to acquire these trappings is made easier by the fact that people, for a time at least, take pride in the kind of public show their representative can make. Only when the cost becomes

On the basis of new archaeological information, Mendelsohn says, "There is good reason to assume that the Samuel account is an authentic description of the semifeudal Canaanite society as it existed prior to and during the time of Samuel and that its author could conceivably have been the prophet himself or a

29

burdensome do they begin to protest. An increase in personnel, forced labor, a system of draft, confiscation of private property, and ever more burdensome taxes, was the route to oppression that Samuel described (8:11-17). In a larger sense, it is a picture of all mankind's servitude because we have chosen the rule of man (and behind him, Satan) over that of God.

spokesman of the anti-monarchical movement of that period."

Israel either did not believe Samuel, or else they thought the prestige of having a king would be worth whatever it cost. They may even have thought they could keep their king under control. At any rate, they refused to back down on their demands, and God told Samuel to let them have their way (8:19-22). They were determined that experience should be their only teacher.

The Lord then led a young man to Samuel who was in outward appearance everything the people wanted in a king. He was striking in appearance, resourceful in a crisis, outwardly modest, and suitably pious—a man after the people's own heart!

I Samuel 9:2; 10:16-24; 11:1-15.

A FAITHFUL GOD
(I Samuel 12)

Even when they failed him, the Lord's faithfulness to His people remained constant. The way He led Saul and Samuel together is just one example of His unfailing guidance. The story is also instructive for us.

Saul had no idea he was about to be anointed king of Israel. He was busy taking care of his responsibilities in the family business. Some asses had strayed away and it was his job to find them. This seems to be the typical pattern of how

Be sure to read I Samuel 9—11 carefully. It is important background for both this lesson and the next.

God calls a man. It is not the one who is sitting around waiting for the big opportunity, but the one who is conscientiously performing the task at hand, on whom He lays His hand. When Saul called on Samuel, it was not with any expectation of honor, but merely because he had exhausted his own resources for finding the lost animals.

In obedience to God, Samuel had anointed Saul to be king (10:1), and Saul had demonstrated his capacity for military leadership by his victory over the Ammonites (chapter 11). Now the time had come for his public acceptance and coronation.

"It is required in stewards, that a man be found faithful" (I Corinthians 4:2). Before turning over the political leadership of Israel (he would continue his spiritual leadership in the office of prophet) to Saul, Samuel justifiably demanded a vindication of his own faithfulness in the office of a judge (12:1-3). All agreed that he had been a righteous judge, taking no bribes and, under no circumstances, using his position to gain any personal advantages (12:4,5).

So conscious was Samuel of his rectitude in fulfilling his functions that he could offer to restore whatever he might be accused of taking unethically (verse 3). Throughout his lifetime in office, he had reflected the faithfulness of the God whose servant he was.

He continued to exercise the office of prophet just as faithfully. On this day of investiture and new beginnings, his duty as a prophet required that he scold the people for their self-will (I Samuel 12:6-12); remind them of their duty to both God and their king (12:13-15); pronounce God's judgment on their sinful behavior (12:16-18); and

> "Saul was willing to ask counsel from God. He was even seeking Samuel to get his help in finding his asses. Let us never think that any service is too menial and insignificant to lay before the Lord. Whatever we do, we have a perfect right to seek guidance from above."
> —Ralph Neighbour

constantly teach, warn, and pray for them (12:20-25).

Samuel and Saul were not the only ones present that day with responsibilities. The people, too, needed to confirm their obligations. They were still the descendants of Abraham, bound to the Lord by an everlasting covenant. Under Moses they had further ratified it. Regardless of the form of government under which they should live, the children of Israel could not abandon their primary responsibility to serve and obey the Lord. They were still required, first of all to heed His commands (12:14,24). Samuel was careful to remind them of this.

Both king and people would fail in their responsibilities to the Lord and to each other. The book of First Samuel contains the sad record of these failures. The Lord, however, would not fail them. He alone is perfectly faithful. Samuel closed his coronation discourse by reminding them that Jehovah their God was the only perfect example of faithfulness. Even if they forsook Him, He would not forsake them (12:22). The "great things he hath done" (12:24) for them included the record of His faithfulness that Samuel had reviewed (12:6-9) as well as all His other great acts in their history. This record was the basis of His claim to their obedience.

Israel needed to be warned, however, that the God who was faithful in bestowing His guidance and blessings was equally faithful when it came to fulfilling the pronouncements and judgments He had recorded against them in the event that they should fail in keeping His covenant (12:25). Because of the thunderstorm with which God had punctuated this day of coronation (12:17,18), they

Genesis 12:1-3; 13:14-17; 15:4,5,13-18; 17:2-19; 22:15-18; 26:2-5,24; 28:13-15; 35:9-12; Exodus 19:1-8; 24:3-7.

Remember, you have verse 24 to *Learn by Heart*.

DISCUSS IT AT
HOME

• Could Samuel
have failed to
impress God's
holy standards on
his sons because
he was so busy
teaching all Israel?
Do we get so
busy in the Lord's
work we neglect
our family
responsibilities?
How can we keep
the two in right
balance?

• Churches are
often plagued
with the problem
of teachers or
other leaders
who hold on to
positions they
can no longer
handle effectively.
How might the
best interests of
these people and
the church be
most kindly
served?

were in an appropriately chastened and repentant mood to take heed of Samuel's solemn
warning (12:19). Yet they were not really expecting judgment. On this festive occasion of a
new beginning, they looked ahead with confidence to a regime of victory and glory.

This was a time of drastic change for Israel,
with far-reaching consequences. They had been a
loose federation of related tribes. There had been
so much individual freedom that the author of
Judges had described their way of life by saying,
"Every man did that which was right in his own
eyes" (Judges 21:25). Now they were to be a nation
under one ruler, regardless of whether he were
wise or capricious. Instead of leadership being in
the hands of men who rose to power under the
impetus of the Spirit of God, and whose creden-
tials were their deeds of valor—regardless of their
backgrounds, Israel would from this time on owe
allegiance to a hereditary king. They would be
subject to him irrespective of whether he followed
the ways of the Lord, or chose his own rebellious
path. It was the beginning of a new era for
Israel.

The career of Israel's first king, like the first
Adam, provides insight into our own fallen
natures. We watch an ideal king—man's ideal—
fall tragically short of God's expectation. Like
Israel, Saul insisted on doing what was right in his
own eyes. Pride, self-will and stubbornness
overshadowed his admirable qualities and led
inexorably to his downfall. In contrast, the
second king was a man after God's own heart and
a picture of the last Adam—Israel's true King.

NOW TEST YOUR KNOWLEDGE

Arrange the following events in the order that they occurred.

A. Saul seeks his father's asses.

B. Saul relieves Nahash's siege of Jabesh-gilead.

C. Samuel anoints Saul captain over Israel.

D. A displeased Samuel prays, and God says it is He who is rejected.

E. The elders of Israel request that Samuel appoint a king.

F. The people ask Samuel to pray for them.

G. God agrees to the people's request for a king.

H. Saul's youthful modesty is shown by his hiding in the baggage.

I. Saul prophesies with the prophets.

J. Samuel installs his sons as judges in Israel.

K. Samuel demands vindication from Israel.

L. Saul hailed as king by the people.

FOOD FOR THOUGHT

"It is God who must reign; . . . and it is to the Lord all kings must look, if they would reign in righteousness and have honour in heaven."—Joseph Parker

SAUL: THE PEOPLE'S CHOICE

I Samuel 13; 15

EVERY DAY WITH THE WORD

Monday	A king's duties	Deuteronomy 17:14-20
Tuesday	Foolish behavior	I Samuel 13
Wednesday	Two with God	I Samuel 14:1-10
Thursday	A great victory	I Samuel 14:19-35
Friday	A foolish vow	I Samuel 14:36-52
Saturday	A kingdom lost	I Samuel 15:1-23
Sunday	Polishing an image	I Samuel 15:24-35

The definition of freedom that men prefer is one which presupposes complete autonomy. Although most men like to believe they have the blessing of a higher power on their efforts, they persist in their desire to seek God and worship Him in their own way. Nevertheless, the freedom they seek is so divorced from a sense of responsibility that when their best efforts fail, they quickly lay the blame on others, and even on the God whose will they have failed to ascertain. Very few accept responsibility with the same understanding evidenced by the late President Truman, who kept on his desk the framed reminder, "The buck stops here."

These twin errors of demand for total independence coupled with refusal to accept total responsibility were first manifested in Adam, and have been basic to our sinful natures ever since. They are deeply involved in the failure of Israel's first king.

THE KING TESTED
(I Samuel 13:1-14)

Surely few have begun their careers with brighter prospects than did Saul. God Himself had pointed him out as the best example of man's ideal king. There was no admired quality he lacked. His physical appearance commanded the utmost admiration. He was gifted with courage and resourcefulness and was valiant in battle, diligent in business, and generous in victory. He was congenial in his relationships, and had reared a splendid son. At the beginning of his career, he had even evidenced an admirable humility and willingness to learn. Perhaps most important of all, he had a prophet of God for his personal teacher and guide. Yet, with all these advantages going for him, he failed. Why?

I Samuel 9:15-17

I Samuel 9:2; 10:24

I Samuel 11:7-11

I Samuel 11:13

I Samuel 9:21; 10:16,22

I Samuel 9:5-8

Someone is supposed to have said about a courageous missionary that he feared God so much he never had to fear man. David, the man after God's own heart, who succeeded Saul—the representative of man's ideal, wrote in one of his psalms, "In God I have put my trust; I will not fear what flesh can do unto me." And in another, "It is better to trust in the Lord than to put confidence in princes."

Psalm 56:4

Psalm 118:9

Saul, on the other hand, became more and more concerned about the image he presented before men and about their continued willingness to accept his leadership. This preoccupation lay at the root of his wrong decisions.

I Samuel 10:8

The first major test of his trustworthiness was one of simple obedience. Samuel, who spoke with the authority of God, had told him that when he faced the enemy in Gilgal, he was to make no move for seven days until Samuel should come to invoke the Lord's blessing by a sacrifice and to instruct him as to how he should proceed in the confrontation.

First Samuel 13:19-23 reveals how desperate the Israelite situation was. They had no iron weapons because the Philistines retained a monopoly on the metal. See note 2 in *New Scofield Reference Bible*, page 335.

It is easy to understand the consternation Saul must have experienced as he waited out those seven days in Gilgal. Although he had been anointed by Samuel and acclaimed by the nation, he still had to prove himself. The resurgence of national pride that had accompanied the proclamation of the monarchy had encouraged the Philistines to amass their forces and subdue the sparks before they ignited a major rebellion.

Such an enemy show of strength struck panic into the hearts of Saul's untried and poorly equipped army. As each day passed without any action, the Philistine forces were increased and those of Israel were weakened because more and more men went AWOL. Saul was neither impressing the Philistines nor exercising moral leadership over his own people. His image as a king who was capable to "go out before us, and fight our battles" was at stake.

I Samuel 8:20

The faith that was not sufficient for patient waiting, was certainly not strong enough to spark courageous faith in his faint-hearted troops. Human reason dictated that the only way to save the situation was to take some decisive action.

This Saul did. He ordered his priests to prepare a sacrifice in order that he might invoke God's blessing on the coming battle. No sooner had he completed the ritual than Samuel arrived and confronted him with his disobedience and lack of faith.

At this point we begin to see more clearly Saul's basic defects of character. A genuine leader assumes responsibility for his actions, but Saul sought to lay the blame for his decision on the Philistines, the deserters, and even on Samuel himself—anywhere but on his own lack of faith and willful determination. Had he at this point confessed to wrong-doing and evidenced genuine repentance, how different his subsequent history might have been.

It is significant that Samuel did not attempt to explain to Saul his delay at arriving in Gilgal. Saul's responsibility had been to obey the directions that had come to him from God regardless of the human circumstances. Saul proved he was not a man after God's own heart, because he had not trusted Him in the crisis. "Without faith," wrote another inspired author many centuries later, "it is impossible to please Him." Hebrews 11:6

That Jonathan, not Saul, became the hero of that first confrontation with the Philistines may be one of the evidences of God's rejection of Saul. I Samuel 14
Certainly, when a crisis developed between father and son over Jonathan's unwitting disregard of the king's rash vow, the people showed clearly that their sympathy lay with Jonathan.

THE KING REJECTED
(I Samuel 15:10-35)

The rash behavior and arbitrary and capricious authoritarianism that Saul displayed in the incidents of chapter fourteen may well have been his reaction to the fiasco of his disobedience at Gilgal. His self-esteem was undoubtedly slipping, and he feared for his hold over the people. One senses an undercurrent of panic in his behavior that betrays his lack of trust in Jehovah. He stands in bold contrast to the faith of his son Jonathan.

How much time elapsed between those incidents and the climactic events of chapter fifteen we are not told. The latter would seem to have been much later in his career.

On this occasion Saul's failure marked his final rejection. Samuel, who had begun his prophetic career with the unhappy task of announcing God's judgment on Eli and his house, now in his old age had to proclaim God's rejection of Saul's dynasty. So greatly did he love the attractive king whom he had shepherded through his career that he spent the whole night in tears (15:11). When the time came to act, however, he pronounced God's sentence with firmness and authority.

The first step was to bring Saul face to face with his sin. He had been ordered to execute Jehovah's vengeance against the Amalekites for their opposition to Israel in the wilderness. Had he been faithful to the duty of a king to meditate day and night in the Book of the Law, he would have known God's intention in the matter even before Samuel told him the duty was to be his. Three times the Lord had recorded His purpose to utterly destroy the children of Amalek.

Saul's disobedience was backed up by a barefaced lie. With the sheep bleating a background denial (verse 14), he brazenly greeted Saul with the announcement, "I have performed the commandment of the Lord" (verse 13). When he could no longer deny his guilt, he resorted to his

"If king Saul represents the best of the flesh, how can we expect him to be a successful warrior against it?"—S. Ridout

Exodus 17:8-16

Deuteronomy 17:14-20

Numbers 24:20; Deuteronomy 25:17-19

customary tactic of blaming someone else (verses 15,21).

A proper meditation on God's Word would have warned the king how seriously the Lord took it when His people demonstrated such covetousness as to keep valuable spoils which He had ordered destroyed. The book of Joshua was undoubtedly in existence as part of the sacred Scripture well before Saul's day. It gave a prominent place to the story of Achan, who kept for himself some valuable spoil from the city of Jericho, although the Lord had ordered it completely destroyed. Achan's fate stands for all time as a solemn warning against a covetousness that would defy the commands of Jehovah. Yet Saul, lacking the moral authority to insure compliance with the Word, sought to lay responsibility on the people he governed, and added self-righteously that they were going to be sacrificed to the Lord (verse 21). There is a significant little pronoun in verse 21. It is not "my God," but "thy God" of whom the king speaks. It sounds almost as if he wants to suggest he is doing Samuel a favor in making a sacrifice to a God to whom he personally owes no allegiance.

Joshua 7

The Word of God through His prophet puts sin in its true light. Stubborn and willful disobedience to the known will of God is the basic sin. It was the downfall of Adam and Eve, and it characterized the whole career of Israel's first king. Saul had been given every opportunity to repent and grow in his relationship to the Lord. Now "rejected" was stamped across his career. From this point on it was all downhill. He would have a career of fighting, and at its climax he would fall in battle against the Philistines.

DISCUSS IT AT HOME

● God's message comes to us today through the Scripture. Why do people often pray for guidance on matters where the Bible has already spoken clearly? Can you think of any circumstances in which an emergency situation justifies ignoring a plain command of Scripture?

● What can we learn from Samuel about being uncompromising about obedience to God's Word while still caring about sinners? How is his behavior a picture of both God's justice and love?

Properly placed faith would have brought victory; instead, misplaced faith brought defeat and death.

The true nature of the king is summed up in his manner of accepting the sentence of God. His concern was not that he had failed in the mission the Lord had entrusted to him, but that the people should not know of his failure and rejection. He is utterly abject in his pleading with Samuel to protect his image before the nation (verses 27-30). To a point the prophet humors him (verse 31), but makes clear God's will by personally dispatching the Amalekite king (verses 32,33). After that he never again goes near Saul (verse 35), though he deeply mourns the loss of so promising a protégé (16:1).

Saul was an able man, abundantly blessed with natural gifts and a great opportunity for service. It is because his abilities and opportunities were not dedicated to the Lord that he failed. It is not possible for anyone to serve Him acceptably with his own unaided assets. "Without faith it is impossible to please him," we read in Hebrews 11:6. All that we are and have must be submitted to His authority and harnessed to His power.

Looking again at God's description of the ideal king in Deuteronomy 17:14-20, we see that the temptations which cause the downfall of kings—to power, to wealth, and to self-indulgence—were those that felled our first parents. The real sin of leaders, like that of all men, is living for self-glory instead of God's glory. Only the Son of God, Israel's true King, completely rejected these temptations. He did so because He had meditated so much on God's Word that He could use it to rout the tempter. This Saul failed to do.

41

NOW TEST YOUR KNOWLEDGE

Fill in the blanks from the words in the list below:

After his victory over the Ammonites, Saul was hailed as king. These events seem to have greatly disturbed the 1)_____ who, it would seem, promptly occupied the central hill country. However, the first blow was struck by 2)_____, Saul's son. In response the enemy collected a large force and camped at 3)_____, in the hill country. When Israel saw the size of the invading army, many fled over 4)_____ into the land of Gad. Meanwhile, Saul rallied what men he could at 5)_____.

Saul waited there 6)_____ days for 7)_____ to join him, but as the time, like his men, began running out, he ordered a burnt offering. No sooner was it done than the prophet appeared and announced that Saul had done 8)_____, a word the king was to echo later in his life. Samuel assured Saul that God sought a man after His own 9)_____. After the sacrifice, Saul and his men went on to 10)_____, which became his capital.

Answers:
a) ten   d) Gibeah   g) wisely   j) seven
b) heart   e) Philistines h) Samuel   k) foolishly
c) Gilgal   f) Jordan   i) Jonathan   l) Michmash

FOOD FOR THOUGHT

"Men of genius are admired; men of wealth are envied; men of power are feared; but only men of character are trusted."

DAVID: JEHOVAH'S CHOICE

I Samuel 17—20

From "Invictus" by William Ernest Henley. The author is said to have died a suicide.

EVERY DAY WITH THE WORD

Monday	God's choice anointed	I Samuel 16:1-13
Tuesday	Accepted at court	I Samuel 16:14-23
Wednesday	In the king's family	I Samuel 18
Thursday	Inroads of jealousy	I Samuel 19
Friday	A loyal friend	I Samuel 20:1-23
Saturday	Forced into exile	I Samuel 20:24-42
Sunday	David's confidence	Psalm 59

"My thoughts are not your thoughts, neither are your ways my ways, saith the Lord. For as the heavens are higher than the earth, so are my ways higher than your ways, and my thoughts than your thoughts" (Isaiah 55:8,9). The story of Saul and David illustrates this. Nowhere in Scripture is the contrast between man's ideal and God's more graphically set forth than here. It seems easier for men to relate to Saul than to David. They can empathize with one who shakes his fist at Heaven and vows at any cost to keep his throne. "I am the master of my fate; I am the captain of my soul," they affirm. They cannot understand one who takes abuse and persecution without retaliating and does not lift a finger to obtain for himself what he firmly believes is his God-ordained destiny. Historical fiction based on this era has presented Saul as a tragic hero and

David a brash opportunist and master of political intrigue who master-minds his sovereign's downfall and his own enthronement.

Only when God's Spirit transforms us into the image of His Son do His values become our values, and our ways begin to approach His ideal.

A MAN AFTER GOD'S OWN HEART
(I Samuel 17)

Saul went down to defeat determined to keep the control of his destiny in his own hands. David yielded up the reins to Jehovah, and has this epitaph for all time, that he was a man after God's own heart. It will be our privilege to follow the shaping process of such a man of God.

Some interesting contrasts can be made with Jacob, who was also chosen by God, and who also knew as a youth God's purposed destiny for him. But Jacob thought he had to help God bring His will to pass, even by foul play, whereas David was content to wait God's time and God's methods. On the other hand, there are striking parallels in David's experiences that mark him as a type of Christ. These are worth watching for as you study.

Genesis 25:29-34; 27

Begin a list of these and be prepared to share them with your class.

We have a few clues as to how David became a hero of faith at so early an age. Many of the long solitary hours he spent with his father's sheep must have been used to study the seasons, the changing panorama of the heavens, the evidences of God's handiwork all around him. At other times he must have often meditated on God's Word. During these years also, he must have practiced making the wonderful music that first

As witnessed by Psalm 8.

See Psalms 19; 119.

44

soothed Saul and in later years led to the great musical heritage that became so integral a part of Israel's worship. There were hours he practiced with his slingshot. Who knows how many predators that small weapon drove off? He learned responsibility and the meaning of trust, regardless of personal cost. In later years after he became king, he viewed himself, not as an ancient oriental despot, but as shepherd of God's flock, responsible for their safety and welfare.

He learned patience. Even after being singled out by Samuel and anointed king, he was content to continue as an obedient son in his father's house, accepting whatever responsibilities were given him, both toward his family and toward his king. Many another lad would have developed a strut at that point, cautioning his older brothers to beware how they treated him, since he would one day be their king.

He learned courage when the sheep for which he was responsible were attacked by wild animals. Risking his life for them, he learned trust. He must have cried to God for help as he rushed toward the lion and bear, since he unhesitatingly gives Him glory for the victory (I Samuel 17:37).

No giant, frightening as his appearance might be (17:4-7), had any more right to the blood of one of God's people than the lion and bear did to the blood of David's father's sheep. If faith and courage could defeat wild animals, why could they not defeat a cursing, blasphemous Philistine? David asked this question of the soldiers (verse 26) and, although his brother publicly belittled him, he put his life in God's hands and offered to take on Goliath (verse 32).

Some stories never grow old. Polycarp's ringing

I Chronicles 21:17. David's revelation of God, immortalized in Psalm 23, must have come out of these early experiences.

"Courage is fear that has said its prayers."—E. Doan

"Saul looked at the giant and thought he was too big to hit; David looked at the same giant and thought he was too big to miss."
—M. Dearnley

45

testimony at the stake: "Eighty and six years have I served Him, and He has done me nothing but good; how can I now deny my Saviour and King?" are as thrilling at the ten thousandth hearing as at the first. Luther's famous "Here I Stand" speech never wears out. Yet they do not top David's wonderful challenge to Goliath (verses 45-48). Read it aloud and picture the setting: on one mountainside (17:3) the unarmed youth, probably unable even to grow a beard (verse 43); one wonders if his voice cracked as he flung his challenge across the valley; on the other mountain the frighteningly equipped giant. One can hear the story from the Cradle Roll to the Golden Age Class without losing its excitement.

Did you learn it by heart?

Nor did the Lord fail His young servant. Before His own backslidden people, and before the heathen Philistines, He vindicated the honor of His Name, and the faith of His champion. His eye was on that tiny missile as it left David's sling, and His hand unerringly guided its trajectory to its vulnerable target. The echoes of David's challenge may still have been ringing against the mountainsides when the fall of the massively armored giant shook their foundations.

The name of Jehovah of hosts (or armies) was the primary weapon David took into the battle; yet the Lord was pleased to use a secondary one— the sling with which he would have gained skill by long hours of faithful practice. Who would have guessed, seeing the boy grow up with his lyre and his sling, that the Lord could use for His glory the latter instrument as surely as He could David's wonderful gift of music? Mission boards say that no training or ability one has is wasted on their fields, and this is equally true in the larger

Do you encourage all your children's interests as possible vehicles of God's glory and service, or do you set up an arbitrary hierarchy of values determined by your own predisposition?

46

realm of God's work. The humblest skill becomes great in His service, if it is surrendered to Him. David soothed a king with his music, and he routed an army with his sling.

PREPARATION OF A KING
(I Samuel 18—20)

David was riding the crest of a great wave of glory. The king was ready to heap honor upon him (17:25,55-58; 18:2). Jonathan, the crown prince, conceived so great a friendship for him that he arrayed him in his own princely habiliments, in effect making him a brother-in-love, and sealing the act with a covenant (18:1-4). The king's daughter fell in love with him (verse 20). And to all the people he was a national hero, praised more highly than the king (verses 5-7).

This is a heady situation for a young man to handle; it is far more likely to prove damaging than is adversity and humiliation. Had David followed the world's way to power, he and his admirers might have marched on the palace and proclaimed him king, the anointed of God to replace the faithless and failing Saul. They might even have persuaded Samuel to lend his authority to the coup. But David was God's man. He had not sought kingship; it was the Lord who chose and anointed him. What He had begun, David was content to let Him complete in His own time and way.

The contrast between man's ideal and God's was beginning to come clearer. Chapter 18 outlines it sharply. It did not take long for Saul to recognize in David the successor prophesied by Samuel, and his natural affection for the valiant

Remember that one of the qualifications for God's ideal king, according to Deuteronomy 17:14-20, was that he eschew the temptations of personal power and prestige by conquest (accumulation of horses) along with other forms of self-indulgence. A rewarding devotional exercise is to consider how our Lord, when tempted (Matthew 4:1-11), demonstrated

young man soured into bitter envy and hatred. Determined to hang on to his throne for himself and his son in spite of Samuel and Almighty God Himself, Saul fast became a slave to fear and to a hatred that would be appeased by nothing less than murder. What an illustration he is of the words of the Apostle John, "Whosoever hateth his brother is a murderer" (I John 3:15). So deep-seated was his rage, that he turned even on his own son and daughter when they protected David from his intentions (I Samuel 20:17,30-33).

While Saul's fears were increasing, David was growing in wisdom. Notice the progression: David "behaved himself wisely" (18:14); "very wisely" (18:15); and "more wisely" (18:30). In David's life all things, even the wrath of the king, were working together for good, both for himself and for the nation. Every time the king sent him out to battle, hoping to see him slain, the enemy became fewer, the nation more secure, and the hero's image brighter.

David had proven himself against the temptations that go with success and popularity, but he was not yet ready to receive the throne. God's man had yet to be refined in the furnaces of adversity.

Inevitably, in view of Saul's increasing jealousy, the time came when it was no longer possible for the young hero to remain at court. When, with the aid of his faithful wife, he escaped ambush and death in his own home, he sought out Samuel for advice and encouragement. Even here, Saul pursued him (19:18-24). Not even the protection of God's prophet and his own faithful old teacher was any longer sacred to the maddened king, so far had the once-promising leader fallen.

that He perfectly fulfilled the qualification. David, remember, is only a type or foreshadowing of God's true King.

David never wavered in his loyalty to his sovereign, who was still in his eyes "God's anointed." Even at this point he would have returned to court and continued his service as one of Saul's loyal officers had the king made the slightest gesture of welcome or reconciliation. Through the devoted Jonathan, he sought to discover whether such reconciliation was possible (I Samuel 20). This friendly errand nearly cost Jonathan his own life (20:33).

It should be noted that Jonathan, though he surrendered to David his own claims to the throne, knowing it was God's will for the nation, was not thereby disloyal to his own father. He remained at court, serving him faithfully. And, although he never joined him in his illegal pursuit of David, he died at the king's side fighting Israel's real enemy, the Philistines (31:2,6; II Samuel 1:23). Furthermore, he demonstrated the highest loyalty to his father's best interests when at great personal risk he sought to persuade him to yield his own ambition to God's will concerning David.

David never again returned to Saul's court. After renewing his covenant with Jonathan, he began to serve the long years of exile where he learned to trust Jehovah as his perfect refuge for every situation. Many of the lessons that he learned in the bitter wilderness school that kept him hidden from Saul are preserved in the Psalms.

DISCUSS IT AT HOME

• Envy is surely one of the hardest giants for even Christians to conquer. Why do we feel resentment when another is preferred before us, gets the promotion we deserved, wins the honor we worked for, is praised for achievements that are ignored in us? How can we gain victory over this giant? Does Jonathan give us a clue?

FOOD FOR THOUGHT

"He always wins who sides with God."

49

NOW TEST YOUR KNOWLEDGE

Answer T (true) or F (false):

1. _____ Samuel thought Eliab looked the part of a king.

2. _____ David saw Goliath when he played the harp for Saul.

3. _____ Saul offered great reward to whoever killed Goliath.

4. _____ David's brothers urged him to volunteer.

5. _____ Saul thought David was too young for the job.

6. _____ David's strength was the name of the Lord.

7. _____ He killed the giant with his fifth stone.

8. _____ Saul's oldest daughter became David's wife.

9. _____ David behaved himself wisely in everything he did.

10. _____ The whole nation loved and praised him.

11. _____ Saul became so jealous and fearful that he finally wanted David murdered.

12. _____ At one point his life was saved only because his wife helped him escape.

13. _____ On that occasion he took refuge with Samuel.

14. _____ Jonathan, although he was Saul's legal heir, remained steadfastly loyal to David. His father came close to killing him for it.

15. _____ David never again returned to court, but was a fugitive until Saul's death.

GOD PREPARES HIS MAN

I Samuel 21—26

Learn by Heart:
"Love your enemies, bless them that curse you, do good to them that hate you, and pray for them which despitefully use you, and persecute you" (Matthew 5:44).

Judges 19:14—21:23. This incident must have occurred early in the period of the judges.

EVERY DAY WITH THE WORD

Monday	Succor in God's house	I Samuel 21
Tuesday	Faithful unto death	I Samuel 22
Wednesday	A vain pursuit	I Samuel 23
Thursday	Touch not mine anointed	I Samuel 24
Friday	Not given to hospitality	I Samuel 25
Saturday	Vengeance refused	I Samuel 26
Sunday	How to lose an enemy	Romans 12:17-21

The tribe of Benjamin was the smallest and least esteemed in Israel. At one point it came very close to being completely exterminated. Yet its history boasts two very illustrious men. Each was named Saul, and each wrote his own epitaph.

The first Saul rose from lowly beginnings to the pinnacle of success, only to fail ignominiously because of stubborn self-will that demanded he hang on to his worldly position at all costs. When he faced himself and summed up his life, he said, "I have played the fool, and have erred exceedingly" (I Samuel 26:21).

Philippians 3:8

The second Saul began with every worldly advantage, but in order to cast his lot with God's Anointed, he "suffered the loss of all things" and counted them "but dung." When he knew that death was imminent, he could review his life and say, "I have fought a good fight, I have finished my course, I have kept the faith: Henceforth there

II Timothy 4:7,8

is laid up for me a crown of righteousness."

Disobedience cost one Saul of Benjamin an earthly crown; obedience won for another an eternal one.

WILDERNESS LESSONS
(I Samuel 22—24)

In the ultimate, every man's destiny is determined by his relationship to God's Anointed. Since Saul and David shared this distinction, their contrasting attitudes to one another and the Lord's corresponding dealings with them is instructive. Saul may be likened to Adam, who was designated head of creation but forfeited this throne by insisting on self-determination. God then began preparation for a King after His own heart (pictured in David). Though Adam (all unregenerate mankind) refuses to yield his sovereignty to God's chosen King, yet that King was willing to become Adam's Saviour. Even as Saul must finally acknowledge David, so must all Adam's race one day acknowledge their rightful King: "Jesus Christ is Lord."

"Anointed" and "Christ" come from the same root word, translated "Messiah" from the Hebrew.

Genesis 1:28; 3:1-6,17-19

I Samuel 24:20; 26:25

Philippians 2:11

But anointing and coronation are not the same thing. David, like our Lord of whom He is a picture, had to follow a path of suffering and rejection between the one and the other.

How imperfect are even God's choicest saints. The boy who could so courageously defy a giant in the name of the living God, the Lord of hosts, still had many lessons to learn of faith and obedience before he was ready to lead God's people. It would appear that his initial reaction to Jonathan's warning was one of panic. There is no record of consideration or planning, much less of

David's description of this experience is preserved in Psalm 34; his relief over his safe escape in Psalm 56.

J. T. Davis (*Birth of a Kingdom*, p. 80) suggests Samuel may have sent Gad to join David and give him spiritual counsel. Samuel, remember, had founded a school of prophets.

turning to the Lord for instruction. David simply fled with no food, no weapon, no destination. He must have had in mind some idea of getting help from the Lord, for he went first to the high priest at Nob. But he did not confide his problem to him and ask counsel from God. Instead he tricked Ahimelech into supplying his need, lied about his situation and then, still following his own impulses, sought asylum with—of all people—a Philistine king!

The Philistines wanted nothing to do with this one who had been so formidable a foe. For all they knew, his tale of a break with Saul was a ruse that he might infiltrate their ranks. If it were true, they could expect Saul's armies to come against them for harboring a traitor. To save his life, David was reduced to playing the fool (21:10-14). In his humiliation he hid in the cave Adullam and, finally, slowed down enough to hear the Lord speak. Psalms 57 and 142 record for us his confession and commitment as he at last turns his troubles over to God and awaits His orders. The Lord then sent him a prophet to reveal the secure hiding place of His choice (I Samuel 22:5).

However, he still had not learned the full consequences of his folly. Back in Gibeah, Saul had learned of Jonathan's covenant with David and the latter's escape. In a rage, he accused the entire court of being in league against him (verses 6-8). At this point, Doeg, an Edomite in the service of Saul who had seen the transaction between David and Ahimelech in the tabernacle, spoke up to exonerate the court by suggesting that the real traitors were the priests (verses 9,10). Enraged, Saul ordered the entire company of the priests— along with their families and livestock—to be executed (verses 11-19). The heir to the high priesthood managed to escape and, with the ephod, hurried to join David (22:20; 23:6). By this time David had collected around him a band of refugees who were, for one reason or another, disaffected by life under King Saul (22:1-4).

David was both conscience-stricken and grief-stricken when he heard Abiathar's gory story. He recognized that he himself must share the guilt for the slaughter of the priests (verses 21-23). For the impious Doeg, however, who had not only betrayed him, but who was ready and willing personally to turn his sword on God's servants the priests (verses 17-19), David had nothing but bitterness and contempt. The words of Psalm 52 call down the Lord's vengeance against one so profane and blasphemous.

Almost immediately we have encouraging evidence that David stopped running blindly and truly turned over the reins of his life to the Lord. Faced with a new decision—an implied request to use his followers to fight off a Philistine attack on the town of Keilah—David sought to know the Lord's will (23:1,2). When his fearful followers thought he must be hearing the Lord wrong, he asked a second time in order to confirm the answer (verses 3,4). Then he stepped out boldly and, to the credit of his men, they did not desert. The result was an encouraging victory at Keilah (verse 5).

If David expected gratitude and protection, however, he was quickly disillusioned. Hearing where he was, Saul started down with an army to besiege the city until they should surrender David. Again David inquired of the Lord before making a decision and, as a result, left the city

The ephod was the garment the high priest wore when acting in his official capacity. See Exodus 28; 39:1-26.

Notice in Psalm 52 that David's imprecation (call for God's judgment) is not directed against God's anointed (Saul), but against Doeg, the upstart, who boasts himself to be a mighty one.

Emile Cailliet (*Journey Into Light*, p. 21) has this beautiful statement: "Christian friendship is an election. We

before Saul could arrive (verses 7-13).

In his new hideout near Ziph, David was greatly encouraged both by Saul's inability to discover him, and by the ease with which Jonathan was able to contact him. His friend brought him food, a renewal of his covenant of loyalty, and confirmation of his understanding that it was God's will for David to be king. The magnanimity, the faith, the self-denial that his act and words required of Jonathan, the legal crown prince, is almost beyond understanding. If Saul is a picture of the old Adam in man, Jonathan, his son, is certainly a picture of the Christian who has honored the principle to deny himself, and follow Christ.

Jonathan's encouragement was timely, for David was soon to suffer another setback when the Ziphites, among whom he was dwelling, betrayed his whereabouts to Saul. His prayer to God in this crisis is recorded in Psalm 54. The answer came in the form of a new Philistine attack against Israel. Saul had to drop his pursuit of David to fight his real enemy.

By this time, David was ready for a major test of his faith. He was resting in the lovely oasis of En-gedi when Saul renewed his pursuit, forcing him to take refuge once again in a cave. There are a great many caves in that area, but Saul chose to rest in the one in which David and some companions were hiding (I Samuel 24:1-3).

Had we been in David's situation, how easy it might have been for us to decide that the Lord had given us this opportunity and it was up to us to make the most of it. In fact, his friends urged this very argument upon him (verse 4). It did not impress the man after God's own heart. God's

Word, which was ever his delight, clearly reserved vengeance to God. It was not man's prerogative. Even less had man the authority to touch one whom God had anointed. David contented himself with demonstrating to Saul that he was not his enemy, and for the moment, Saul showed himself contrite.

VENGEANCE AND TWO FOOLS
(I Samuel 25; 26)

Saul's brief moment of wisdom lasted long enough for him to call off his pursuit of David and go home. The death of Samuel and the national mourning observed for him no doubt further restrained the king from any overt acts of aggression for a time (I Samuel 25:1).

During this interval of freedom, David used the opportunity to strengthen his position as champion of his own tribe, Judah. The area to which he retired was one where the wealthy sheep herders grazed their flocks. It was wild country where the roving herds and their keepers were in constant danger of raids by nomadic peoples or the ever-hostile Philistines. David took it upon himself to police and protect this territory (verses 7,14-16). It was a necessary task, and he had a right to expect that he and his followers would be given sustenance by the owners of the herds in return for his protection. Therefore, when one of these owners came into Carmel to oversee the shearing, David sent some of his men to pay a call and receive his provisions (verses 4-8).

Nabal must have been a thoroughly despicable character (verse 3). His very name meant fool, and both his servants (verse 17) and his wife (verse 25),

If you have maps in the back of your Bible, trace David's movements for greater appreciation of the hardships of his years of exile. Anyone who hopes to become a serious Bible student should acquire a good Bible atlas for one of his basic tools.

called him a son of Belial. His servants were afraid to approach him on the subject of his own danger (verse 17), nor did his wife consult with him before taking action, or tell him about it until a day later (verse 37). She proved to be as wise as her husband was foolish, not only saving Nabal from the reward of his own folly, but saving David from the sin of personal vengeance (verses 32-35).

God showed approval of David's timely repentance by removing Nabal and giving David his wealth along with the lovely Abigail (verses 37-42). The description of Nabal's last hours (verses 36-38) reminds us of the rich fool of Luke 12:16-21 who, within hours of his death, rejoiced over his accumulation of earthly goods.

DISCUSS IT AT HOME

● Can we use the Bible prohibitions against personal vengeance to apply to lawful judicial processes?

Meanwhile the self-willed Saul had forgotten his better intentions, mustered his army, and renewed his pursuit of David. We know from Psalm 54 that David again sought God's help. With only one companion, he stole into Saul's sleeping camp and helped himself to the king's weapon and water jug. Abishai, David's aide, sought permission to assassinate the king, but David restrained him in words that expressed firm faith that his just cause would be upheld by His God (I Samuel 26:5-12). For the second time he openly convinced Saul he had no designs against his life. This time the chastened king appears to have abandoned his futile crusade for good (verses 13-25; 27:4). Yet his days were as surely numbered as Nabal's. Recognition of "playing the fool" came too late.

NOW TEST YOUR KNOWLEDGE

The following places are associated with David's years of exile. After each one write what occurred there.

1. Adullam _____

2. Carmel _____

3. Engedi _____

4. Gath _____

5. Gibeah _____

6. Keilah _____

7. Mizpeh _____

8. Nob _____

9. Ramah _____

10. Ziph _____

FOOD FOR THOUGHT

"Sweet are the uses of adversity."
—William Shakespeare

TRAGIC END OF SELF-WILL

I Samuel 27—31

EVERY DAY WITH THE WORD

Monday	David's confidence	Psalm 27
Tuesday	A year with the enemy	I Samuel 27
Wednesday	Saul's despair	I Samuel 28
Thursday	Preparation for battle	I Samuel 29
Friday	David spared treason	I Samuel 30
Saturday	The king is dead	I Samuel 31
Sunday	David's testimony	Psalm 37:1-20

"The Lord seeth not as man seeth" (I Samuel 16:7) contains many facets of truth. For example, human inclination is to make its heroes all virtuous and its villains beyond hope. Thus we take it as a personal affront when our "good guys" reveal their feet of clay, and we put the worst possible constructions on any worthy motions made by our "bad guys."

This is not God's way. He readily lets us see the qualities we can admire in a Saul. He is handsome, able, resourceful, brave, persistent. David, on the other hand, is pictured as impetuous, quick-tempered, backsliding, lustful. By worldly standards, Saul was at least as good a man as David.

I Samuel 16:7

"But the Lord looketh on the heart." He looked into the heart of Saul and saw pride. Saul would always be concerned about his image, his control of men and circumstances, his ability to be master of his own fate and by his own efforts achieve his own way. All this was more important to him than was obedience to the Word of God.

David, however, wanted God's will above all else. When he strayed from that path, he was ever ready to repent and return to the right way. Nowhere is this difference between the two men more clearly depicted than in the final crisis of Saul's reign.

SELF-WILLED BEHAVIOR
(I Samuel 27—29)

After their final confrontation, Saul abandoned his vain pursuit of David (I Samuel 27:4). David, however, did not trust Saul, which in itself is scarcely surprising. His years of youth and vigor were fast receding and Saul appeared to be as firmly settled on the throne as ever. The years of exile and uncertainty appeared to stretch on endlessly. "I waited patiently for the Lord," David later wrote in Psalm 40:1. But in this instance, at least, his patience appears to have wavered. Without consulting the Lord, he decided he would be better off serving one of the Philistine princes than remaining in Judah and trying to dodge King Saul (I Samuel 27:1-3).

He had made this mistake at the beginning of his exile and Achish had refused to give him asylum. Now Achish must have decided that David's estrangement from Saul was permanent and that he would make a loyal ally to himself. In return for David's supposed services in ridding his borders of enemies, presumably marauding Israelites, Achish gave David a substantial piece of property on which to settle with his followers (verses 5,6).

For over a year (verse 7) David lived there and

I Samuel
21:10-15

Is it too much to suggest that David was for a time guilty of serving two masters?

"If we believe not, yet he abideth faithful: he cannot deny himself"
(II Timothy 2:13).

I Samuel
22:16-19; 25:1

walked the edge of a razor. He cleared the territory of Judah of the nomadic groups that remained from the Canaanite peoples, winning much favor thereby with his own tribe. At the same time he allowed Achish to believe his forays were against the people and territories of Judah (verses 8-12). Even during his backsliding, God was protecting His anointed king. Never once did a suspicion of the truth come to the ears of Achish. He was, in fact, ready even to add David's contingent to his forces when he prepared for that last great battle against Saul (28:1; 29).

One wonders what went on in David's heart as he faced this dilemma. To appear reluctant to accompany Achish would have undone all the impression he had been working so hard and so dangerously to build up. On the other hand, to go to war against the people over whom he had been anointed king, and especially Saul, against whom he had sworn never to lift his hand because he was "the Lord's anointed," was unthinkable. David must have passed some hours in anguish as he realized what lay at the end of the road he had taken when he consulted with his own heart (I Samuel 27:1) instead of with the Lord.

Saul, meanwhile, was in even greater anguish. He saw the size and strength of the Philistine forces mustered against him, sensed that the end of his own rebellious path was fast approaching, and appeared to realize for the first time that his stubborn self-will had shut the door of Heaven against him. He had nowhere to turn. Samuel was dead, and he himself had ordered the massacre of the whole company of priests, causing the legal high priest to join David with the ephod which represented his authority to mediate the message of God to man.

Very well, if the divinely constituted lines of communication were shut off from him, Saul would make use of the forbidden ones. In obedience to the divine condemnation, Saul had rid the nation of all who practiced the occult professions (I Samuel 28:3). Now, however, he sought information as to where one such practitioner might still be found, and, traveling incognito, he made the long arduous journey to consult her. On arrival, he demanded to be put in touch with Samuel (verses 7-11).

The tenor of the text seems to support the thesis that it really was Samuel who appeared on this occasion. There is no suggestion that the witch even began the seance, but rather that Samuel appeared immediately after Saul's demand. The terror of the woman would not make sense if her own accustomed rituals had produced the expected results. Furthermore, the words of Samuel are not the lying words of a demon, but a confirmation of all God had already spoken through him to Saul. He repeated what Saul already knew, that the Lord had turned against him. Samuel reminded Saul of the words of judgment spoken on the occasion of his disobedience concerning the Amalekites that his kingdom would be given to another (verses 17,18). Then he added what Saul wanted—and didn't want— to know. The coming battle (the very next day) would result in defeat for Israel and death for Saul and his sons (verse 19).

Overcome by hunger and fatigue, and recognizing at last the immutability of the Lord's decrees, the old king collapsed in a faint (verse 20).

I Samuel
22:20-23; 23:6

Leviticus 19:31;
Deuteronomy
18:9-12

For God's
prohibitions
against our
dabbling in the
occult, see
Leviticus
19:31; 20:27;
Deuteronomy
18:9-12; Isaiah
8:19,20; I Timothy
4:1; Revelation
21:8. For the Holy
Spirit's decisive
comment on
Saul's deed, see I
Chronicles 10:13.

I Samuel
15:23,26,28,29

SELF-WILL'S CONSEQUENCES
(I Samuel 30; 31)

Meanwhile, behind the Philistine lines, David was experiencing the bitter taste of rejection. The Philistine leaders overruled the desire of Achish to have David and his men among his forces. In this respect, they showed far more insight than did the king of Gath. Although David made a proper show of reluctance, there must have been great relief in his heart as he marched his men away from the arena of the coming battle (chapter 29).

On arriving back at Ziklag, however, he faced a scene of horror and devastation. The city was burned out and plundered. His wives and the wives and children of all his men were gone. In their grief, the men who had been so faithful to him under long and difficult circumstances, blamed him for the tragedy. They were actually on the verge of stoning him (I Samuel 30:1-6).

In his extremity David cast himself on the Lord (verses 6-8). He had been permitted to travel the whole bitter road and see the end of following the advice of his own heart. Now he would see how his God could bring victory out of defeat, glorify His name and protect the one who put his trust in Him. After seeking divine guidance, David and his company set out after the raiders, perfectly assured of victory (verses 9,10).

They were successful. "David recovered all" (verse 19), the Scripture says simply. Not only did he recover all that he and his men had lost, but also sufficient spoil from the defeated Amalekites to amount to considerable wealth. So much was it that it almost cost a civil war in his own ranks. He

Read Psalm 119:67,71. Could the affliction that taught David to pay close heed to God's Word be a reference to this experience of chastening?

An example of how abundantly "all things work together for good to them that love God, to them who are the called according to his

63

had taken two thirds of his men with him, leaving as guards the remaining two hundred who, on that occasion, were physically unable to fight (verse 10). Covetous over the riches they had plundered from the enemy, the fighting force was determined not only to keep it all, but even to deny the inactive two hundred men the return of their own possessions with the exception of their wives and children (verses 21,22).

David's fitness to be king is nowhere better attested than at this point. Alone, he denounced their greed over what had been the Lord's blessing, and suggested that the suitable way to express their thanksgiving for safety and victory was with fair-mindedness. All would share equally, he pronounced, regardless of their particular duty in the enterprise. And this became the rule in his kingdom (verses 23-25).

He put his own share of the spoil to good use by sending gifts to the leading men of all the cities of southern Judah (verses 26-31). It was an astute political move, undoubtedly advancing his image as their natural leader. The greatest good, however, to arise out of the tragedy at Ziklag was that David and his company were far from the action, and any possibility of recrimination, during the great battle that ended in Saul's death.

Whatever else he may have been, Saul was as brave a man as he was determined. With God's judgment of doom ringing in his ears, he made the long journey back to his camp, doggedly taking his place with his sons in the forefront of the battle (I Samuel 28:25; 31:1). Then, wounded and defeated, his sons (including Jonathan) lying dead around him, Saul ended his life by his own hand. He died as he lived—ruled by his pride. He

purpose" (Romans 8:28). Not only did David's grievous chastisement restore him to reliance on the Lord, but it resulted in gain where there had appeared to be loss.

would not survive to become the plaything of the victorious Philistine princes as had Samson (31:2-4).

There is a touch of grace at the end of this tragic life, suggesting the love and loyalty Saul was capable of inspiring, and thus giving a hint of the leader he might have become. The citizens of Jabesh-gilead had not forgotten his great service to them in rescuing them from certain humiliation at the hands of the Ammonites. At considerable personal risk, they rescued the bodies of the king and his sons from Philistine irreverence and gave them a decent burial (verses 11-13). David, after he became king, was to take personal note of this act of devotion.

Saul, whose career began with so much promise, died a failure. The reason is that he had no faith in God, trusting rather in his own reason. Even when he sought God, as in the forbidden offering at Gilgal or the forbidden consulting of the dead, it was rather to force the Lord to bless his chosen way rather than to seek God's will for his next step.

David was no greater than Saul when it came to physique, or astuteness, or bravery, or resourcefulness, or ability to lead an army into battle against the nation's enemies. In only one respect was he greater—he had faith and confidence in the Lord. He was willing to place his hopes and his life unreservedly into the hands of an invincible and just and loving God who would never deceive him or forsake him. This is what makes a man after God's own heart. "Without faith it is impossible to please him." The passage you are to learn by heart sums up how Saul and David illustrate this.

DISCUSS IT AT HOME

• Depression, or discouragement, is a common problem even among Christians. What have you found to be its causes? Cures? Can it be prevented? How?

NOW TEST YOUR KNOWLEDGE

Who said it? (Answers may be used more than once.)

1. There is nothing better . . . than to speedily escape into the land of the Philistines.

2. Give me a place . . . that I may dwell there.

3. Where have ye made a road today?

4. Know assuredly that thou shalt go out with me to battle.

5. Seek me a woman who has a familiar spirit.

6. Why hast thou deceived me? For thou art Saul.

7. Why has thou disquieted me to bring me up?

8. Behold thine handmaid hath obeyed thy voice and I have put my life into my hand.

9. Is not this David, of whom they sang to one another in dances?

10. My master left me because three days ago I fell sick.

11. Behold a present for you of the spoil of the enemies of the Lord.

12. Draw thy sword and thrust me through.

a) Achish
b) Samuel
c) the princes of the Philistines
d) David
e) witch of Endor
f) Saul
g) Gad
h) David, in his heart
i) Jonathan
j) young Egyptian

FOOD FOR THOUGHT

"My times are in thy hand; who saith 'the whole I planned,' Trust God, see all, nor be afraid."—Robert Browning

8
GOD TIMES DAVID'S CAREER
II Samuel 1:1—5:5

Learn by Heart:
"The steps of a good man are ordered by the Lord: and he delighteth in his way. Though he fall, he shall not be utterly cast down: for the Lord upholdeth him with his hand. I have been young, and now am old; yet have I not seen the righteous forsaken, nor his seed begging bread"(Psalm 37:23-25).

I Samuel
21:10; 27:1

EVERY DAY WITH THE WORD

Monday	News for David	II Samuel 1:1-16
Tuesday	David's elegy	II Samuel 1:17-27
Wednesday	Civil war	II Samuel 2
Thursday	Abner's perfidy	II Samuel 3:1-21
Friday	Joab's revenge	II Samuel 3:22-39
Saturday	Ish-bosheth's end	II Samuel 4
Sunday	To everything a time	Ecclesiastes 3:1-8

The memory verse for this lesson is taken from the heart of a psalm in which David extols the peace and fulfillment that are the lot of one who puts his trust in the Lord and waits patiently for Him to guide his next step. The first eight verses, which sum up the heart attitude of the one who lets the Lord lead his life, begin and end with the admonition to "fret not." In between he uses the positive imperatives of trust, delight, commit and rest.

As we have seen, David himself did not always follow this excellent advice. He, too, was human and wayward. But as he came more and more to experience the blessings that resulted when he did commit his way unto the Lord, he learned not to fret and rush at situations his own way. Thus, out of the crucible of his personal experiences he

67

has given us this psalm which has comforted and steadied so many.

A TIME TO PLANT
(II Samuel 1:1—2:7)

The Lord guides our steps aright, because He has a proper time for everything in our lives and He alone knows when that time is. We do not, and He has forbidden us to unveil that He has hidden. No witch of Endor is commissioned to raise that veil. It would be the very opposite of the trusting, delighting, committing and resting that develops the working muscles of our faith.

Deuteronomy 18:10-14. See footnote 1 in *New Scofield Reference Bible*, p. 238.

When news came to David that Saul had been killed in the battle of Gilboa, he did not promptly and eagerly rush to Gibeah and declare himself the legally anointed successor. His first act was a judicial one, however. He executed the Amalekite who, having boasted of relieving the king of his misery, brought the symbols of kingship to David in the hope of rich reward (II Samuel 1:13-17).

Gibeah was the place of Saul's palace.

His second act was to honor the fallen ruler with an elegy unparalleled for its beauty and magnanimity (II Samuel 1:17-27). All Saul's admirable qualities and accomplishments are commemorated, and his failures forgotten. David made it an official item in the mourning rites of Judah (the only tribe in which his authority was accepted at this point).

There is a poetic justice in Saul breathing his last by the hand of an Amalekite. It was his disobedience of God's command to utterly destroy the Amalekites that led to his rejection as king (I Samuel 15:16-23).

Having done all he could for the memory of his predecessor, David then turned to the Lord and asked to be shown his next step (II Samuel 2:1). The response was that he was to go up to Hebron. He and his six hundred followers settled there with their families, and there the elders of the tribe met together and confirmed him as their recognized king.

Hebron was an appropriate choice. Not only was it a leading city in the territory of Judah, but it had an illustrious history. Abraham had built his first altar there. It had become a center of worship and a principal place of abode, not only for him, but also for Isaac and Jacob. Here Abraham was buried in the cave he had bought for Sarah's interment. At the time of the conquest of the land under Joshua, Caleb (who was then prince of the tribe of Judah) had asked for it as his family inheritance and then, although he was eighty-five years of age, wrested it from the possession of the giants.

Genesis 13:18; 23:17-20; 35:27

Joshua 14:6-14

David's first recorded act after this official recognition is again significant. He commended the people of Jabesh-gilead for risking their lives to rescue the bodies of Saul and his sons from abuse by the Philistines, and giving them a decent burial. He promised to reward their faithfulness, and made it clear that he coveted such loyalty in his own ranks (II Samuel 2:5-7).

I Samuel 11:1-11; 31:11-13

Saul had, at the beginning of his reign, rescued Jabesh-gilead from certain destruction by the Ammonites. Though a whole generation would have grown up since that event, gratitude for their deliverance had evidently been kept alive in their hearts.

A TIME TO REAP
(II Samuel 2:8—5:5)

There were still eleven tribes to be won over before David would, in fact, be king of Israel.

Even though it was common knowledge that the Lord had chosen him, there were rebels still determined to have their own way. Chief among these, of course, was the house of Saul, Saul's relatives, and his tribe—Benjamin. Abner, Saul's general, proclaimed Saul's surviving son, Ish-bosheth, king and established him safely in Mahanaim, east of the Jordan (II Samuel 2:8,9).

In the long and bloody civil war that followed Saul's death, David is not in the limelight. Instead, the focus is on the two opposing generals, both forceful and interesting characters, surprisingly alike, yet bitter foes.

Abner had been commander-in-chief to Saul, probably for most of his reign. He was the king's uncle and unswervingly devoted to his interests. After David's victory over Goliath, it was Abner who had formally presented the young hero to Saul (I Samuel 17:57). During the time David was winning fame for his military exploits for Saul, he and Abner must have become well acquainted. We know that these two were the only ones besides Jonathan to sit at the king's table (I Samuel 20:25). It may be that Abner became jealous of David's military genius and his position as the king's son-in-law, fearing that David posed a threat to his own status. This may have increased his willingness to serve Saul as faithfully in the pursuit of David as in the pursuit of the Philistines. How humiliated he must have been when David taunted him openly in the king's presence for so failing in his duty as Saul's protector that his weapon and water could be stolen from beside him. The rankling memory might well have spurred him on in his resolve to thwart David's rise to the throne of all Israel.

Ish-bosheth may not be his real name since it means "man of shame." Since "bosheth" (shame) is often substituted for "Baal," he probably is the Esh-baal (fire of Baal) of I Chronicles 8:33.

Remember how the women had sung, "Saul hath slain his thousands and David his ten thousands" (I Samuel 18:6,7).

I Samuel 26:15,16

Note that when Nathan was condemning David's taking of Bath-sheba, he listed among the evidences of God's favor hithertofore the fact that God had given David Saul's harem (II Samuel 12:8).

Compare I Samuel 26:6 and I Chronicles 2:16.

I Kings 2:28-34

James Pritchard, who excavated at el-Jib, believes he uncovered the actual pool of Gibeon where the battle of II Samuel 2:13-16

That Abner was also personally ambitious must be inferred from his relationship to Ish-bosheth. This unheroic son of Saul seems to have been Abner's pawn rather than Abner being his servant. Abner acted as regent even though Ish-bosheth was forty years old (II Samuel 2:10). Neither would Abner have taken Saul's concubine, Rizpah (II Samuel 3:7), had he truly respected Ish-bosheth's position as king for, according to oriental usage, the harem of a deceased king was the inviolate property of his legal successor. So sure had he become of his position and authority that his pride would not tolerate a rebuke from his puppet (verse 8). His cause was by then all but lost, but this episode gave him the excuse he needed to seek a peace treaty with David (verses 9-12).

Joab was David's nephew. He is not discussed in the history until this time, yet he must have been one of the six hundred who followed David in his exile, and had so proved himself as to become chief of his armed forces. Though ruthless and unprincipled in many ways, he was unswervingly loyal to David. He had no compunction about openly disagreeing with the king on occasion, and David seems to have handled him cautiously. Joab held his position through David's entire reign, then was executed by Solomon because he had supported the accession claims of Adonijah.

Hostilities between the rivals opened at Gibeon when they agreed to decide the issue through a trial by combat. It was similar to the rationale of the battle between David and Goliath. In this instance, however, twelve combatants were selected from each army with the understanding that each was to try to plunge his sword into the side of his opposite number while they held headlocks on each other. When all twenty-four fell dead, a general battle ensued, and the forces of Benjamin were put to flight (II Samuel 2:12-17).

As Abner fled, he was followed by Asahel, Joab's brother, who evidently realized that if he could slay Abner the war would be virtually over. He was young, and such an act would make him a name. Thus, when Abner sought to dissuade him from personal combat, he refused (verses 18-23). Although Abner wanted no blood feud with Joab, he was left with no choice but to kill his pursuer in self-defense.

This battle of Gibeon is the only one between the rival armies that is recorded in detail. Joab's forces appear to have won a decisive victory (verses 30,31), yet we are told that the war continued for a long time (II Samuel 3:1). This would not imply constant fighting, but rather sporadic outbreaks with no settlement of grievances until the defection of Abner.

Although Joab had no personal designs on the throne, he was too jealous of his position as commander-in-chief to brook a potential rival. Although his treacherous slaying of Abner (II Samuel 3:26,27) was due primarily to the blood feud that existed between them because of Asahel's death, a second motivating factor was undoubtedly his fear of so powerful a rival who had the loyalty of eleven of the tribes. David would not have found it easy to have both these men in positions of influence at his court.

It is interesting to notice that David did not summarily dispose of Joab for his deed as he had

was fought. He says: "The most spectacular monument discovered in four seasons at el-Jib is the large pool with a spiral staircase, hewn from the bedrock of the hill just inside the wall on the north east side of the city.... The cutting of this landmark of ancient Gibeon involved the quarrying and removal of approximately 3,000 tons of limestone, much of which was undoubtedly used in the construction or the rebuilding of the city wall which runs beside it. How long it must have taken to carve out this hole, 80 feet deep, cannot even be guessed." *Gibeon, where the Sun Stood Still*, pp. 64-5. On p. 160 he adds, "We have found that ... the area around the great pool at El-Jib was completely free of buildings. There would have been sufficient room in the open

72

square for the two dozen men who were involved in the contest as well as for a considerable number of spectators."

the Amalekite who beheaded Saul, and later the two slayers of Ish-bosheth (II Samuel 4:5-12). Either he relied heavily on Joab, or he feared repercussions from his family, or he recognized the blood feud right of the next of kin to avenge the shedding of blood. He did, however, make his abhorrence of Joab's treachery so unmistakably plain that he was able to retain the loyalty of the eleven tribes that Abner had so recently brought under his sway (II Samuel 3:31-39).

There is much in these chapters that people find offensive to Christian moral standards. There are those who will throw them at you as their excuse for not believing the Bible and accepting Christ. We must not lose sight of the fact that the Scripture which gives us these incidents is the same Word of God that gives us the standards by which we are judging them. The fact that the Holy Spirit has recorded them does not imply that God either ordered or approved them, only that they are true history. He is telling us that man, sinful as he is, can still have a relationship with the Lord provided only that he trust and delight himself in Him and commit his ways into His keeping. Such a man God will use, and lead, and delight in.

With Abner and Ish-bosheth both dead, there remained no one around whom the eleven tribes could rally. They formalized their acceptance of David. Thus, God's time having come, the prophecy of Samuel was at last fulfilled, and David ruled as king over all Israel (II Samuel 5:1-5).

NOW TEST YOUR KNOWLEDGE

Arrange the following events in chronological order:

1. a) The Amalekite brings news to David of the outcome of the battle of Gilboa.

2. b) Abner breaks with Ish-bosheth.

3. c) David is anointed king over Israel.

4. d) Death of Saul.

5. e) David's lamentation.

6. f) Joab murders Abner.

7. g) Battle of the pool of Gibeon.

8. h) David moves to Hebron.

9. i) Abner proclaims Ish-bosheth king of Israel.

10. j) Judah anoints David their king.

11. k) Ish-bosheth murdered.

FOOD FOR THOUGHT

"Can a man have real success apart from the conviction and fact that God is guiding his life?"—Philip E. Howard

GOD ACCEPTS DAVID'S WORSHIP

II Samuel 5:6—6:23; 8

EVERY DAY WITH THE WORD

Monday	God's love for Jerusalem	Ezekiel 16:1-14
Tuesday	God's place of meeting	Exodus 25:10-22
Wednesday	Victory and a capital	II Samuel 5:6-25
Thursday	A center of worship	II Samuel 6
Friday	Peace secured	II Samuel 8
Saturday	Jerusalem's king comes	Luke 19:28-46
Sunday	Jerusalem's future	Zechariah 8:1-8

It is in keeping with the rebellious nature of sinful man that we are so often prone to behave as if we thought we were doing God a favor when we perform any act of worship. In popular parlance, we applaud the ideal of "every man finding his own path to God," or "worshiping God in our own way." Even Christians, who rightly approach God through His Son, become guilty of handling the things of the Lord in a light or profane way, allowing long intimacy to inure them to a proper sense of His holiness.

Even David had to learn that neither ignorance nor good intentions are an acceptable substitute for knowing and doing God's will in the way that He has ordained. A holy God makes the rules by which a sinful people may come into His presence.

GOD GIVES HIS PEOPLE PEACE
(II Samuel 5:6-25; 8)

The most loved, the most prayed for, the most fought over city in all the earth is Jerusalem. The adherents of three great faiths have considered its streets the most sacred soil in the world. Through the centuries their armies have fought each other for possession of it; this in spite of the fact that the name means "foundation of peace."

It was David, under the inspiration and guidance of God, who made Jerusalem the center of Jewish aspiration and the symbol of Christian certainty, first by his capture and development of the city and then by the glorious psalms that through the centuries have carved its name and meaning in devout hearts.

John, in his Revelation, associated the new Jerusalem with the bride of Christ, the church (Revelation 21:2). Like the church, it had no merit of its own, being one of the strongholds of the heathen Canaanites until the king redeemed it for himself in a bath of blood and made it holy (II Samuel 5:6-10). After it became his, he beautified and glorified it (verses 9-12) and made himself at home there (verses 12-16).

Ezekiel plays on this theme of its original lack of holiness when he upbraids the city (and through it the nation) for committing abominations against the One who had so desired and purified it, saying, "Thus saith the Lord God unto Jerusalem; Thy birth and thy nativity is of the land of Canaan; thy father was an Amorite, and thy mother an Hittite" (Ezekiel 16:3). Archaeological discoveries have amply illustrated this heathen background of the holy city. The earliest

Besides Christians and Jews, Muslims consider Jerusalem holy because Muhammed is supposed to have been taken to Paradise from the place on Mount Zion where their sacred mosque now stands.

Compare I Corinthians 3:16.

So named because they contain denunciations.

reference to Jerusalem comes not from Genesis, but from execration texts found in Egypt. Along with some other Palestinian cities, its name was inscribed on a human-like figurine (dated to shortly after 2000 B.C.) intended for use in ceremonies of black magic. The theory was that as the figurine was shattered, so would Pharaoh's enemies be broken.

From the fourteenth century B.C.—the era when Egyptian authority over Syria-Palestine was weakening—comes correspondence written on clay tablets which the diggers uncovered at the Egyptian capital of Tell-el-Amarna. Seven letters to Pharaoh are of interest to us because they came from Abdi-Hiba, king of Jerusalem, and describe his struggles against the Habiru, who many think to be a reference to the invading Hebrews. It was from this background that David "redeemed" the city and caused it to be called by his own name and be looked on as holy.

Psalm 2; Isaiah 9:6,7; Joel 3:20,21; Zechariah 2; 8.

See also I Chronicles 11:1-9; 12:23-40; 14:1-17.

That the holy city, the "foundation of peace" continues to have a history of warfare is due to the fact that its rightful King is not in residence there. God's recipe for peace on earth is for His appointed King, accepted by all His people, to rule from His appointed city. So it was in type when the man after God's own heart set up his throne in Jerusalem to the united acclamation of the chosen nation, there was peace in Israel. The Philistines who had held them in vassalage from the days of the judges were at last defeated (II Samuel 5:17-25; 8) and the nation was to enjoy an era of unprecedented peace and prosperity.

GOD ENFORCES RIGHT WORSHIP
(II Samuel 6)

David had something more in mind for Jerusalem than an outstanding and well-fortified seat of government. It was also to be the center of religious activity, the site of the nation's corporate worship.

From the time the people had left Egypt, the Lord had insisted that they have one center of worship, one place where they would meet with Him and offer the sacrifices that symbolized repentance and atonement. This place was at the ark of the covenant where the stone tablets that held God's demands for man's holiness were covered by the mercy seat whereon was sprinkled the blood of atonement for man's sinful failures.

Deuteronomy 12:5-21

Exodus 25:21,22; 40:20; Leviticus 16:13,14; Numbers 7:89. The "testimony" refers to the tables of the law.

When Israel settled down in Canaan, the ark was set up in Shiloh, but as the backsliding of people and priesthood increased, the ark was profaned until it was treated as a mere fetish. The sons of Eli carried it into battle where it was captured by the Philistines and then returned because of their superstitious fear of it. Then it was set aside, having rested for a whole generation on the property of Abinadab. Since the tabernacle was at Nob until Saul slaughtered the priests, and the great altar at Gibeon, Israel's worship was not being carried on in the manner prescribed by Moses.

David's first step in making Jerusalem the center of worship was to move the ark there (II Samuel 6:1,2). In his zeal, however, he failed to consult the Lord. Instead of learning from His law how the sacred furnishings and implements should be handled, David took his cue from the practice of the world. The Philistines had transported the ark on a new cart and it had worked quite well. The procession, complete with band,

Exodus 25:10-22; Numbers 4:1-15

I Samuel 6:7-16

was assembled and started on its joyous way (verses 3-5). Alas for David's man-made plans, the festival ended abruptly when Uzzah, who was tending the ark, put forth his hand to steady it and immediately fell dead (verses 6,7).

Uzzah's sudden end was a harsh but necessary reminder that Israel's God was holy and the things pertaining to Him must not be profaned. This contrast between His holiness and man's sinfulness is the basic theme of the whole law. That He may be worshiped only in the way He decrees is constantly reiterated. David, whose responsibility as king included study of God's Word (Deuteronomy 17:16-20), the priests who were responsible for the things of God, and Uzzah himself in whose family the ark had been cared for twenty years, should all have known God's instructions concerning it.

David was resentful, even fearful, at this tragic judgment. For three months he left the ark at a temporary resting-place until he had made a study of God's law concerning its handling (verses 8-11).

Joy was still the keynote when the procession to Jerusalem was finally renewed, but this time it was a joy mixed with reverence and care for God's order. The king himself led the parade and joined wholeheartedly in the festivities and sacrifices— much to the chagrin of his wife, who seemed to feel that the dignity of the royal family was being undermined (verses 13-18). He closed the festivities with a generous serving of refreshments to the whole multitude (verse 19).

That would have been a nice note on which to close the account; however, the day did not end too happily for David. When he returned to the

DISCUSS IT AT HOME

• Are there things done in our church that border on impiety or profane the things of God? If so, suggest ways of correcting them.

• Are we ever justified in serving God by methods other than He has ordered because of the nobility of our motives or the importance of our purpose? If we

palace, his wife Michal berated him for what she considered his unseemly display of exuberance. Knowing he had been right, David rebuked her attitude, and the Lord confirmed it. Michal was to remain childless (verses 20-23).

feel that the judgment on Uzzah was too severe, does it suggest we lack appreciation for God's holiness?

FOOD FOR THOUGHT

"The duty which God requireth of man is obedience to His revealed will."
—Shorter Catechism

NOW TEST YOUR KNOWLEDGE

Choose the best answer:

1. Until David, Jerusalem was controlled by the a) Arameans; b) Philistines; c) Phoenicians; d) Jebusites.

2. In the Bible, Jerusalem is called by all these names except a) Zion; b) Salem; c) Moriah; d) Nebo; e) City of David.

3. The defenders of Jerusalem felt so secure that they claimed their walls could be defended by the a) women and children; b) sick and the dead; c) lame and the blind.

4. David's men surprised the defenders by entering through the a) aqueduct; b) gutter (water shaft); c) secret gate; d) power gate.

5. After capturing Jerusalem David made it his a) offering to God; b) military post; c) capital.

6. In building his palace, David had the help of a) Hiram of Tyre; b) Nathan the prophet; c) the Philistines; d) Nahash of Ammon.

7. At the first attempt the ark was carried on a) the backs of oxen; b) a new cart; c) the shoulders of priests; d) the shoulders of chosen tribal leaders.

8. God's method for carrying it was on a) the backs of oxen; b) a new cart; c) the shoulders of priests; d) the shoulders of chosen tribal leaders.

10
GOD REWARDS DAVID'S MOTIVES
II Samuel 7

EVERY DAY WITH THE WORD

Monday	God's mercies to David	Psalm 32
Tuesday	The Davidic Covenant	II Samuel 7:1-17
Wednesday	David's response	II Samuel 7:18-29
Thursday	The King announced	Luke 1:26-35
Friday	The Davidic Kingdom	Micah 4:1-8
Saturday	The King's enthronement	Zechariah 14:9-17
Sunday	Psalm of the Covenant	Psalm 89:1-4, 20-37

Learn by Heart: "He shall be great, and shall be called the Son of the Highest: and the Lord God shall give unto him the throne of his father David: And he shall reign over the house of Jacob for ever; and of his kingdom there shall be no end" (Luke 1:32,33).

However loudly we proclaim our faith, most of us find it all too easy to accept the Lord's refusals as being disappointments rather than stepping-stones into His larger and more glorious purposes. Yet, in hindsight this is what they prove to be.

A woman wanted to go to the mission field, but after several boards rejected her, she became convinced that such was not the Lord's will. She married, reared several children, made her home a center of missionary interest and support in addition to entertaining them frequently. She lived to see every one of her children leave that home for a mission field.

Thus does the Lord often turn our desires to uses we do not suspect at the time. He did so with David and David's faith was great enough to accept the disappointment with joy as he contemplated the greatness of God who had in mind something more wonderful for him than he himself could have dreamed.

THE DAVIDIC COVENANT
(II Samuel 7:1-17)

The arrangement of the books of Samuel does not always appear to be a chronological one. The prophet who wrote it seems interested in developing each theme before proceeding to the next. It is, therefore, not always easy to fix events in an exact order in David's reign.

We are not told how much time had elapsed since the capture of Jerusalem and the bringing in of the ark. There had been time to negotiate with King Hiram over the purchase of lumber and the hiring of expert craftsmen, and to have built a magnificent palace for the king's own residence. The back of Philistine resistance had been broken (II Samuel 7:1), but we know that David was never able to be fully a man of peace, so it must have been a quiet period between wars. He was still riding the crest of God's favor and the nation's hero worship.

David never did learn how to use idle time. As he wandered about his newly completed palace, his mind was already contemplating new projects. The beauty of the house, which represented the epitome of Phoenician art and know-how, must have contrasted sharply with the simplicity of his childhood, his nights as a youth sleeping on the hillsides with his sheep, and his days of hiding in caves as he fled from Saul. As he reached his roof, he could see the tent he had erected on the crest of Mount Zion to hold the ark. Overwhelmed with all the evidence of God's favor to him, he was shamed by the thought that he should dwell in a building more magnificent than that designated for the place of God's residence among His people. His poet heart began to conceive a house truly worthy to be the dwelling-place of the One who had done so much for him. He would attempt to correct the incongruity of having lavished so much wealth and beauty on himself while doing so little to beautify the house of God.

Shouldn't more Christians look about the homes the Lord has given them and say, "What more can I do for the Lord's house and the Lord's work?" No doubt we would see great growth in His business.

To his credit, David did not run straight to Hiram with a new order for materials and masons. Instead, he first consulted with God's prophet, Nathan. This chapter is our first introduction to this bold man of God. Of his loyalty to David there is no doubt, but his first loyalty is firmly with the God for whom he spoke. He quickly encouraged David to put his plan in motion (verse 3), no doubt reasoning that it was a worthy one, that it was intended for the glory of God, and that the Lord had blessed the king in all his undertakings.

Nathan figures importantly in our next lesson. Later (I Kings 1:5-40) he is God's instrument to fulfill His purpose to place Solomon on the throne in spite of the ambitions of Adonijah, Joab, and Abiathar.

But that night Jehovah visited Nathan, and he was faced with the embarrassing prospect of withdrawing his approval. His experience should warn us that even men of God may err in their understanding of His will. Much friction in Christian organizations would be avoided if leaders did not insist on equating their own best reasoning with "thus saith the Lord," and humbly submit to knowing the Lord's will without regard to whether it is their own way or another's that prevails.

An example that may be mentioned is that of Paul and Barnabas (Acts 15:36-39), who could not agree on the extent to which John Mark should be disciplined for his failure in their mission.

The Lord gave Nathan two reasons why David should not build the temple. First, He reminded David that He had dwelt in a tent from the time

Israel had left Egypt. Then He pointed out that He had never asked any of the tribes to build Him a permanent dwelling. During their long history in Canaan under the judges, various tribes had been ascendant at different times, yet the tabernacle had remained at Shiloh until its destruction in the time of Samuel. Then the worship was centered at Nob and Gibeon. In effect, God was reminding David that the conquest was not over and it was not appropriate to build a permanent temple until the nation was fully at peace. David's job was to complete the wars.

The Lord next reminded David of His past blessings, reviewing his history from a shepherd boy sought out by Samuel to his present position on the throne of all Israel. During all those years He had been with David and already had made his name great in the earth (verses 8,9).

Next God, still through the mouth of Nathan, reviewed His promises to Israel—a perpetual land of their own with peace and security from all their enemies (verses 10,11).

Finally, God made a series of promises to David: his kingdom would survive with a dynasty that would last forever (verses 11,12); the son who would succeed him would have a kingdom and throne that would last forever, regardless of his personal worthiness (verses 12-16).

David's son Solomon did succeed him and did build the temple of which David dreamed. And even though he sinned and thus lost much of the kingdom for his descendants, Jerusalem remained in the hands of his dynasty.

But this was not the real fulfillment of Nathan's prophecy. David's throne would last forever because in his lineage would be born the Heir so

We have no record of any greater king or empire in the tenth century B.C. Before and after that time there were great empires in western Asia that made Palestine their battlefields.

long promised to Abraham—the Messiah of Israel and Redeemer of mankind. He would be chastened with the stripes of men because the iniquity of men would be borne by Him, but after that He would sit on "the throne of his father David: and . . . reign over the house of Jacob for ever; and of his kingdom there shall be no end." The coming of that day is as certain as the promises of God.

Isaiah 53:6

Luke 1:32,33

As if to emphasize that the real thrust of the prophecy is the Messiah, the words "for ever" are used in the passage, not once, but three times (II Samuel 7:13,16). We find it emphasized still further in the psalm of Nathan the Ezrahite, where we read: "His [David's] seed shall endure for ever, and his throne as the sun before me. It shall be established for ever as the moon, and as a faithful witness in heaven."

Psalm 89:36,37

ACCEPTED BY DAVID
(II Samuel 7:18-29)

David realized he was being designated the forebear of the Messiah as shown in Psalm 110 and our Lord's use of it. In deep humility he voiced recognition of his absolute unworthiness of such a privilege and the greatness of the God who had bestowed it (II Samuel 7:18-22).

Matthew 22:41-46

As king and representative of the nation, David thought back over its history and reviewed the blessings that had come upon them. That the destiny of the people was bound up with that of the throne and the Messiah, he already understood. It was not their worthiness—for they had failed their God many times—but the Lord's faithfulness that would enable them to continue

DISCUSS IT AT
HOME

• Humility is one
of the most
unpopular of
Christian virtues,
often mentioned
scornfully. What
is its place in the
Christian's life? Is
there a true and a
false humility? Do
you see a
relationship
between true
humility and
gratitude?

as a nation forever with God Himself, in the person of His Messiah, to rule over them from His throne in Jerusalem (verses 24-26).

"Do as Thou hast said" seems to be the gist of the closing words of David's prayer. More in keeping with its tenor is the suggestion, "I know that Thou shalt do as Thou hast said." From that moment David knew the absolute security of his lineage and his throne and the nation's destiny, because he knew the faithfulness of the God who gave the revelation. "Thou has revealed" (verse 27); "thy words be true" (verse 28); "thou . . . hast spoken" (verse 29). David was not asking that the promise be kept; he was accepting it as a gift already bestowed. Just that certain can be our reliance on every promise of God.

FOOD FOR THOUGHT

"When God withholds one blessing, He has a way of granting another, and that more glorious."—A. W. Blackwood

NOW TEST YOUR KNOWLEDGE

Fill in the blanks:

1. David thought it an embarrassment that he should dwell in a _____ while the ark of God dwelt in a _____.

2. Therefore he proposed to _____, the prophet, that he build a suitable house for Jehovah.

3. Although the prophet's first reaction was _____ _____, God spoke to him in a _____ _____, forbidding David to carry out his ambition.

4. He reminded David that since the children of Israel came out of Egypt He was accustomed to walking in a _____ and had not at any time _____.

5. After enumerating His blessings on David and on Israel, he promised the king a secure _____ and _____.

6. He promised David that his kingdom would last _____.

7. This promise is known as the _____ _____ and has its fulfillment in _____ _____.

8. David's prayer of acceptance is noteworthy for its _____.

11
GOD PARDONS DAVID'S SINS
II Samuel 9—12

EVERY DAY WITH THE WORD

Monday	A penitent's cry	Psalm 51
Tuesday	Unmerited grace	II Samuel 9
Wednesday	Rejected kindness	II Samuel 10
Thursday	The progress of sin	II Samuel 11
Friday	The consequences of sin	II Samuel 12
Saturday	The source of forgiveness	I John 1:8—2:6
Sunday	The joy of forgiveness	Psalm 32

Satan is not very original in his battle plans. All temptation follows the same path so closely that we are without excuse when we fall into it. It is the pattern that led Adam and Eve to plunge us into its morass and which Satan tried on our Lord (Genesis 3:1-6; Matthew 4:1-11). It is summed up in I John 2:16 as "the lust of the flesh, and the lust of the eyes, and the pride of life," and Christ demonstrated for us the secret of overcoming it with the sword of the Spirit.

The pattern repeated itself in David's downfall, and he, too, was without excuse. As king, one of his obligations was to spend much time in the Word of God. His psalms give much evidence that he fulfilled this obligation. He even taught his people that the blessed man was the one who took time to "meditate day and night" in God's law (Psalm 1:2). Yet at this point in his career he

Deuteronomy 17:18-20

See especially Psalm 119.

appears to have been less able to conquer with the sword of the Spirit than with the fleshly one that had subdued so many Philistines.

David's experience has much to teach us about recognizing temptation, responding to it, and finding forgiveness and restoration when we fail.

THE CAUSES OF SIN
(II Samuel 10:1—11:4)

The prophetic writer has been showing us David in the most ideal terms. His personal character is illustrated in chapters nine and ten. Profound loyalty motivates his grace toward Mephibosheth. Out of gratitude he offers kindness to a neighboring monarch and when it is rejected insultingly is careful to show consideration for the sensibilities of his envoys.

At the beginning of this Scripture David was at the peak of his career. His enemies had been subdued and his kingdom made secure (II Samuel 10). His capable officers were able to lead the army to victory without him. He had been fighting the Lord's battles from his youth, and was inclined now to enjoy the fruits of success. So David took a vacation (II Samuel 11:1).

There is nothing in itself wrong with taking a vacation. Our Lord took His disciples apart to "rest a while" after a busy preaching mission (Mark 6:31). David's mistake appears to have been one of timing. It was "a time of war." There was still a pocket of resistance among the Ammonites and the season of the year was the most fortuitous for a military attack. But David was unwilling to give up the comfort of his

Take time to familiarize yourself with these events and make note of the ways in which they speak to you. Sunday School time is inadequate for exhaustive Bible teaching. Learn to mine its treasures for yourself.

Ecclesiastes 3:8

Perhaps as a child you were taught the famous couplet of Isaac Watts: "Satan finds some mischief still, For idle hands to do."

To what extent has a woman responsibility for a man's sinful thoughts if she is careless about exposing herself? Is contemporary attire inflammatory?

beautiful cedar palace in Jerusalem.

Satan knew David was ripe for attack. He had time on his hands and was both idle and restless. In Palestine the palaces, or chief houses, were always built on the most prominent hill of a city where they had the maximum advantage of the summer breezes from the sea. From his vantage point, therefore, David could see whatever transpired on rooftops all over the city. Unfortunately, what he saw so intrigued him that he failed to avert his eyes. He kept on looking.

"There is no harm in looking," people say. They are wrong. Our Lord said, he that "looketh on a woman to lust after her hath committed adultery with her already in his heart" (Matthew 5:28). David's downfall is an example. His look soon became so covetous that the king who knew the law, "Thou shalt not covet thy neighbour's wife" (Exodus 20:17), failed to meditate on it but instead made inquiries as to the woman's identity (II Samuel 11:3).

By this time David had so thoroughly settled in his mind what he was going to do that even the information that he was coveting the wife of one of his faithful generals did not give him pause. His conscience should have been shouting, "Thou shalt not commit adultery," but if it did, he had found a way to silence it.

The hardships of the wilderness had proved to be less a source of temptation to David than did the luxuries of the palace. Being "at ease in Zion," basking in comfort, wealth and prestige, left the king ripe for the "fiery darts of the wicked one." The same old pattern manifested in the garden of Eden—looking, desiring, and tasting—reasserted itself in David's downfall.

Were we but more alert to recognize it, all sin makes the same appeal. The Apostle John summed it up as "the lust of the flesh, the lust of the eyes, and the pride of life" (I John 2:16). In His wilderness encounter with Satan, our Lord demonstrated for us the secret of victory over all these avenues of temptation. He routed Satan by countering every attack with "the sword of the Spirit, which is the word of God." What comfort His experience should be to us! Not only does it show us the secret of victory, but it reminds us that we need not despair even when we fail, for "we have not an high priest which cannot be touched with the feeling of our infirmities; but was in all points tempted like as we are, yet without sin" (Hebrews 4:15). With this assurance, we can "come boldly unto the throne of grace ... and find grace to help in time of need" (Hebrews 4:16) from the only One who can truly "succour them that are tempted" (Hebrews 2:18).

While in no way condoning David's lustful look and the sequence of behavior that followed, we cannot ignore or exonerate the behavior of Bath-sheba. She could not have been unaware of the situation of her house in relation to the palace. Either she was very careless or was deliberately flaunting herself. Neither is there any evidence that she offered any objections to the king's messengers or sought to dissuade him from his intent. David was quite capable of heeding an appeal to his conscience, as the incident of Nabal has already shown (I Samuel 25:25-34).

David did not intend his affair with Bath-sheba to be more than an incident. He returned her to her home, evidently thinking that what Uriah did not know would not hurt him.

Matthew 4:1-11; Ephesians 6:17. Review Christ's wilderness temptation, remembering that Matthew presents our Lord as Israel's true and ideal King, of which David was only an imperfect type. David learned, too. He wrote, "Thy word have I hid in mine heart, that I might not sin against thee" (Psalm 119:11).

However, on another occasion she showed herself as peculiarly unperceptive. First Kings 2:21 describes how she delivered to her son Solomon Adonijah's request to marry one of David's concubines. Solomon rightly saw it as his rival's next step to claiming the throne.

THE CONSEQUENCES OF SIN
(II Samuel 11:5—12:31)

"Be sure your sin will find you out" (Numbers 32:23). It was not long before Bath-sheba knew she was with child (II Samuel 11:5). As king, David was responsible to uphold the law, and the law prescribed death as the punishment for adultery. Furthermore, his act would appear all the more heinous in that the man he had betrayed was one of his trusted generals, at that time out fighting the battle from which David had taken a vacation.

Leviticus 20:10

He had indulged the lust of the eyes and the lust of the flesh; now the pride of life had him in its grip. For the sake of his public image, David chose to attempt a cover-up. He would find a pretext to bring Uriah home for a night or two and he would never know the child was not his (verses 6-8).

Uriah, however, was either self-disciplined to an unusual degree, refusing even when drunk to enjoy his home while his men were risking their lives (verses 9-13); or else he was more than a little suspicious. The latter seems quite likely since one can hardly believe there was no gossip between the servants of the two households.

In desperation, David then resorted to murder. By Uriah's own hand he sent orders back to Joab that would expose Uriah to the most dangerous area of the battlefront. Joab, as loyal to his master in deceit as in legitimate service, carried out the orders, and Uriah fell in the battle (verses 16,17). The cover-up had worked. When David received the message of success, he observed the proper rites of mourning for his lost general, and then married the widow (verses 19-27).

But David could not hide his sin from One. The God who had been his lifelong shepherd loved him too much to allow him to remain long in so miserable a situation. According to the description of David's wrestlings with conscience as he recorded it in Psalm 32, he was far from being at ease during the months that followed. Yet it was some time after the birth of his child that he surrendered.

Notice that David "had it made" as far as human exposure or penalty was concerned. On this level men do sometimes seem to "get away with" their sins. Do they ever really?

When He knew His servant was ready to repent, God sent the prophet Nathan to bring him to his knees. His pointed parable of the stolen ewe lamb led the king, indignant at such treachery, to pronounce his own judgment. So miserable a sinner deserved death as well as the necessity of paying fourfold for his stolen sheep (II Samuel 12:1-6).

The fourfold judgment was in keeping with the provisions of the Mosaic law, see Exodus 22:1.

At that point Nathan drove home the lesson and pronounced against David the judgment he had decreed for the sinner of the parable. He would never see peace in his day, those of his own house would turn against him, and his own wives would be defiled (verses 8-12). All this was fulfilled in the treachery of his own sons that culminated in the civil war brought on by Absalom's attempted usurpation of the throne.

The pronouncement is threefold at this point. The fourth penalty is not brought out until verse 14, for reasons we shall see.

At last the "drought of summer" that had so shriveled the king's spirit was broken. Humbly he confessed his sin (verse 13) and acknowledged that far above the wrong done to Bath-sheba or Uriah, or to Joab whom he had made an accomplice, or to Israel who was deprived of an able general, he had sinned against a holy God. "Against thee, thee only, have I sinned, and done this evil in thy sight" (Psalm 51:4).

Psalm 32:4. The full expression of his repentance is preserved in Psalm 51. Be sure to read both these psalms in preparation for the lesson.

94

No sooner had David's lips uttered the sincere confession than forgiveness was extended. According to the law and David's own pronouncement, he deserved to die for his deed, but God was merciful and the king would live to fulfill the purpose for which he had been called (II Samuel 12:13). Nevertheless, David would not escape the temporal penalties that had been pronounced against him. God's holiness demanded that His wrath against such flagrant flouting of His commandments be manifested. David's sin had not been so secret as he thought (verse 14). The immediate judgment—that would make the sentence fourfold and guarantee the fulfillment of all the prophet had said—would be the death of the ill-begotten child.

For seven days David fasted and prayed for his son's life (verses 15-18). When the child died, however, he refused to mourn "as those who have no hope." He knew God was just (verses 20-23; compare verse 23 with I Thessalonians 4:13) and he honored Him with his words of testimony.

The Lord again blessed His forgiven servant. He and Bath-sheba, now legitimately David's wife, had more children, including Solomon, his successor, and Nathan, the ancestor of Christ (II Samuel 12:24,25; compare with I Chronicles 3:5 and Luke 3:31). The army meanwhile had continued the siege of Rabbah, from whose walls had come the missile that felled Uriah. The Lord now gave them victory with the result that the Ammonites recognized David as their ruler and were no longer a menace to Israel (II Samuel 12:26-31).

Thus David knew the joy of cleansing and restoration. How clearly we hear his relief and

DISCUSS IT AT HOME

• Increased leisure and retirement seem to make yielding to temptation easier. How can we best handle the benefits of success without succumbing to its dangers?

• Was God unjust

gratitude in the opening words of Psalm 32: "Blessed is he whose transgression is forgiven, whose sin is covered. Blessed is the man unto whom the Lord imputeth not iniquity, and in whose spirit there is no guile."

to take the baby for the parents' sin? What makes us so prone to question or blame God in the midst of trials or griefs?

NOW TEST YOUR KNOWLEDGE

Fill in the blanks from the answers below:

Unable to forget Jonathan's friendship, David sought out his heir, 1. _____ , to share his own table. Similarly, he tried to show kindness to 2. _____ , new king of Ammon, because of his father 3. _____'s friendship. But the Ammonite king thought David wanted an excuse for 4. _____ , and provided one. Soon the Ammonites were confined to their capital, 5. _____. When the war resumed in the spring, David sent his commander, 6. _____ to continue the siege, while he himself tarried in 7. _____. One evening he observed from his rooftop a beautiful woman and desired her. He learned she was 8. _____, wife of 9. _____ , one of his generals. When she became pregnant, David tried to solve the problem by arranging the general's death and marrying her. Then God sent 10. _____ , the prophet, to bring him to repentance.

Answers:

a) war   f) Abigail   k) Gad
b) Rabbah   g) Uriah   l) Bath-sheba
c) Rabath-Giliad   h) Hanun   m) Mephibosheth
d) Nahash   i) Nathan
e) Jerusalem   j) Joab

FOOD FOR THOUGHT

"Moments of leisure are more to be dreaded than those of strenuous toil."—F. B. Meyer

GOD PROTECTS DAVID

II Samuel 13—20

Psalm 3 is specifically ascribed to David's flight from Absalom. Psalm 4 is not, but its general tenor is so similar that they should be studied together.

EVERY DAY WITH THE WORD

Monday	The source of security	Psalms 3 and 4
Tuesday	Absalom's rebellion	II Samuel 15
Wednesday	David's humiliation	II Samuel 16
Thursday	A traitorous friend	II Samuel 17
Friday	Grief and triumph	II Samuel 19
Saturday	Songs in the night	Psalms 62 and 63
Sunday	Messiah's kingdom	Luke 19:11-27

Do you recall times when an insoluble problem or an inconsolable grief made your bed "rocky" and kept you restless through the long, dark hours of the night. What comfort to you then was the memory of David's confident assurance in Psalm 3:5: "I laid me down and slept; . . . for the Lord sustained me"; or perhaps the conviction of Psalm 4:8: "I will both lay me down in peace, and sleep: for thou, Lord, only makest me dwell in safety"?

These psalms and several others are generally believed to have been written during the period of David's flight from Absalom. Like those we looked at which were inspired by his precarious life as a refugee from King Saul's court, they express a confidence and assurance in the overruling power and goodness of the Lord that has made them a source of comfort and strength to the people of God in every era since David's time.

GOD'S JUDGMENT IS SURE
(II Samuel 13:1—17:29)

The immediate source of David's trials, as with so many parents, lay in the attitudes and behavior of his children. It was not an arbitrary fiat of God that the judgment for his sin with Bath-sheba would rise out of his own household; but confirmation of His own moral law that the sins of the father shall be visited upon the children and "as is the mother, so is her daughter." It was not the least of David's grief for his own sins that he had to see the weaknesses that produced them bear fruit in his sons.

Exodus 20:5; 34:7; Numbers 14:18; Deuteronomy 5:9; Ezekiel 16:44

Amnon, his firstborn and heir apparent, displayed all the sensuality that had led to David's own downfall and, like David, the mistaken presumption of royalty that what he wanted he had a right to take.

What Amnon wanted was his half-sister Tamar. She and Absalom her brother seem to have possessed a physical beauty and charm that attracted universal admiration. They must have been patrician in their bearing and thoroughly at home in the ways of royalty, for not only had they been reared in a palace, but their heritage on their mother's side was also royal. She had been a daughter of the king of Geshur.

Amnon's story in II Samuel 13 and Absalom's exile and restoration in chapter 14 are not listed in the Bible readings for the week due to lack of space. Nevertheless, they should be read.

When Absalom learned from Tamar what had happened, he gave her shelter and let his hatred for Amnon grow daily. The king, too, was angry but when, after two years, he had meted out no punishment, Absalom took matters into his own hands and arranged his brother's assassination.

Absalom was the king's favorite. David appears to have grieved more at losing the presence and

The Septuagint text adds to II Samuel 13:21: "Yet he would not grieve the spirit of his son Amnon because he loved him as his firstborn."

companionship of this son during the years of his exile, than he did over the death of Amnon and the tragedy that befell Tamar.

Like Amnon, Absalom's pride led him to believe he was above the law and could take what he wanted. But whereas Amnon's desires turned toward self-indulgence, Absalom was inordinately ambitious. One senses that his zeal to avenge his sister was quickened by the realization that it was Amnon who stood between him and the throne. Even with Amnon disposed of, he could not wait the process of time that would give him the kingdom by orderly succession, but determined to grasp it immediately by deceit and treachery. In this he did not follow the example of his father's early years when he refused to take part in any act of disloyalty toward Saul, but his more recent one when he stamped roughshod over the rights of others in order to legitimize his deeds and their consequences. With the easy cynicism of youth that is so quick to cry "hypocrisy," Absalom did not see the deeper wells of David's heart that could mourn over his own sins and repent deeply while casting the whole weight of confidence on the mercy and love of his God. He saw only the disparity between his father's words and his father's deeds.

Amnon was unfit to rule the people of God because he was thoroughly sensual and self-indulgent; Absalom was unfit because he was thoroughly profane. He was disloyal to David both as son and subject, and contemptuous of the citizenry (II Samuel 15:1-6). He had no compunctions about taking the Lord's name in vain (verse 7), or profaning his father's harem (II Samuel 16:21,22). The removal of these two sons was a

Absalom was not born until after these events. See II Samuel 3:2,3.

"In Amnon's sin David beheld the features of his own unbridled passions; and in his murder by Absalom, two years after, David encountered again his own blood-guiltiness. Absalom's fratricide would never have taken place if David had taken instant measures to punish Amnon. But how could he

judgment on David as Nathan has prophesied; but it was also an evidence of God's mercy on His people Israel.

Absalom's usurpation of the throne was a source of deep and public humiliation to David. If he were to spare the city from the sword, he had no choice but to flee, abandoning his beautiful cedar palace for the rocky comfort of the wilderness (II Samuel 15:14). It was in this situation, not knowing at what moment the emissaries of his disloyal son might come upon him and kill him, that David fell asleep in the confidence expressed in Psalms three and four.

As an added grief, David was made to believe that Mephibosheth, who had been the beneficiary of his unmerited favor because of his deep love for Jonathan, had turned traitor (II Samuel 16:1-4). Another leading member of Saul's tribe, Shimei by name, openly cursed and abused the unhappy king, pelting him with stones as he and his followers hurried out of the city. David's humility of spirit and trust in the Lord to vindicate him are nowhere more clearly seen than in his refusal to let any of his followers silence Shimei (verses 5-13). Finally, with those who had been closest to him rallying to the banner of Absalom, David was forced to rely on the hospitality of men who had been his enemies (II Samuel 17:27-29). As on a previous occasion when his outlook appeared hopeless from the human viewpoint, "David encouraged himself in the Lord his God."

allot that penalty to his son's impurity which he had evaded for himself? (Lev. xviii.9-29). Nor could he punish Absalom for murder, when he remembered that he, a murderer, had eluded the murderer's fate."
—F. B. Meyer

I Samuel 30:6; cf. II Samuel 16:12

GOD'S MERCY IS UNFAILING
(II Samuel 18; 19)

Hushai was apparently too old to help David, so the king urged him to pretend to help Absalom in order to frustrate any good advice Ahithophel might give.

Absalom, meanwhile, appeared to be riding the crest of success. He was in possession of the capital city, the tribe of Judah had rallied to his cause, and he appeared to have in his ranks his father's two wisest counselors: Ahithophel who was really a traitor to David (II Samuel 15:31; 16:13-23; 17:23); and Hushai, a spy (15:32-37; 17:1-16).

When it came to choosing between the conflicting advice of these two, Absalom's real character stood out clearly. Where Ahithophel outlined the course to a quick, sure, and relatively bloodless victory; Hushai appealed to the young pretender's vanity and desire for pomp and public glory. Absalom's cause was lost when he listened to Hushai, thus sacrificing what advantages were in his favor.

David, meanwhile, had not forgotten the arts of war he had so long practiced. Taking advantage of the intelligence he received from his sources inside the city, he rallied his forces and, led by Joab, they routed the attackers (II Samuel 18:1-8).

Be sure to read chapter 18 in its sequence.

Absalom himself perished ignominiously at the hand of Joab, who dared to put political and military reality above the express command of the king (verses 5,9-15). Then, instead of lying in the tomb Absalom had raised as a monument to his own pride, his body suffered a final humiliation; the soldiers cast it into a pit and covered it with stones (verses 17,18).

There was, however, no joy in Israel that night. So great was the king's grief over the death of Absalom that the victory celebration was turned to mourning. The people could express their sympathy only by mourning quietly in their tents (II Samuel 19:1-4). Inwardly, there must have

"The concluding words of Chapter 18 should be a sober reminder to all believers that sin has far-reaching and tragic

been stirrings of resentment that Joab recognized. Instead of honoring his loyal supporters for their victory, the king was ignoring them and dwelling on his grief for his treacherous son. Joab, astute as ever in serving his master's interests, saw that David's subjects could not long sustain their sympathy with a leader who put his personal loss above his nation's triumph. He dared, therefore, to rebuke the king sharply. David, humble in success as in adversity, saw the justice of his general's complaint and roused himself to his responsibilities (verse 8).

David's restoration to the throne was an occasion of unparalleled magnanimity. To his own tribe of Judah, who had been altogether too eager to rally to the support of Absalom, he sent word offering them the privilege of taking the lead in escorting him home. To Amasa, who had been Absalom's military leader, he offered a pardon and the leadership—in place of Joab—of his own military forces (verses 11-15).

The triumphant procession toward Jerusalem was soon joined by a contingent of the leading men of Benjamin led by the impious Shimei who had been so bold in his castigations of the king in his hour of defeat and humiliation. Now he is utterly abject in pleading for his life. In pardoning Shimei, David made the occasion of his return a day of general amnesty for all offenders (verses 18-23).

Mephibosheth, too, met the returning monarch with protestations of his unswerving loyalty, contrary to the allegations of his servant, Ziba. Although the text appears to support the conclusion that Mephibosheth was telling the truth in the matter, David refuses to sit in judgment

consequences. Surely David did not anticipate uttering the words recorded in verse 33 when he engaged in adulterous acts with Bath-sheba. The pitiful cries of David are a solemn warning that there is a price attached to sin and disobedience."
—John J. Davis

Loyal and capable as he was, Joab never seems to have been secure in the king's regard.

against anyone on this day with the result that the servant Ziba fares rather well (verses 24-30).

The account of the aged Barzillai is probably the most touching example of unswerving devotion to the king that asked nothing in return except the joy of seeing his master rightly honored. Barzillai had been one of the foreign subjects who out of his own wealth had cared for the king and his followers in their flight (II Samuel 17:27-29). In gratitude, David sent for him to join the victorious procession and become a member of the king's household.

Barzillai, however, was not interested in forfeiting his independence for the luxuries of the palace. After personally joining the king's escort, he took leave of him, but left Chimham—who was probably his son, as Josephus suggests—to represent him at court (II Samuel 19:31-40).

David never forgot Barzillai and his kindness. Looking ahead to I Kings 2:7, we learn that on his deathbed the king charged Solomon with the perpetual care of Barzillai's household.

In great contrast to David's show of conciliation was the behavior of many of his followers. Jealousy broke out between Judah and the other tribes because of the king's show of favor. This led to a final upsurge of rebellion that gave Joab an opportunity to dispatch his latest rival, Amasa, and to show himself once more indispensable to David as a military leader (II Samuel 19:41—20:23).

Thus through one more crisis God's mercy had upheld and vindicated His servant. The fires of judgment had burned hotly over David, but he had come through them triumphantly in the mercy of God who would not forsake him forever.

DISCUSS IT AT HOME

• David on several occasions experiences very deep grief; for example, at the death of his dear friend Jonathan; at the illness and death of his infant son; and over the deaths of Amnon and Absalom. Some of his psalms also express his grief at the betrayal of his "familiar friend" Ahithophel. Comforting one at such times is a task we all face but never find easy. How can a

103

"Before I was afflicted," David wrote, "I went astray: but now have I kept thy word" (Psalm 119:67).

Christian best help friends and relatives through such difficult periods?

NOW TEST YOUR KNOWLEDGE

Arrange the following events in the order they occurred:

1. a) Absalom restored to David's court.

2. b) David raises an army east of Jordan.

3. c) Amnon's crime

4. d) David flees Jerusalem.

5. e) David restored to Jerusalem.

6. f) Absalom's flight

7. g) Absalom's revenge

8. h) Absalom wins the hearts of the people.

9. i) David mourns the death of Absalom.

10. j) Joab uses a woman of Tekoah to restore Absalom to Jerusalem.

11. k) Joab's army defeats Absalom's.

12. l) Absalom hailed king in Hebron.

FOOD FOR THOUGHT

"Forgiven men may have to reap as they have sown."—F. B. Meyer

GOD HONORS DAVID'S LIFE

II Samuel 22—24

EVERY DAY WITH THE WORD

Monday	End of Saul's house	II Samuel 21:1-14
Tuesday	The Philistine conquest	II Samuel 21:15-22
Wednesday	God's goodness and mercy	II Samuel 22:1-28
Thursday	His kindness to David	II Samuel 22:29-51
Friday	David's final psalm	II Samuel 23:1-7
Saturday	Catalog of heroes	II Samuel 23:8-39
Sunday	Place for an altar	II Samuel 24:1-25

There is only one acceptable sacrifice for sin, and only one altar where man may meet God on the basis of that sacrifice. Christians know the place is Calvary. The entire Old Testament was written in order that we might be prepared to understand that altar and that sacrifice.

Israel failed to understand the lesson, and that has been their tragedy. They did understand, however, that an acceptable sacrifice can be offered to God in only one place, and that must be a place that He Himself chose. For that reason they have offered no sacrifice since the destruction of their temple in A.D. 70.

The law of Moses said that when the people entered the land they were to have one place that the Lord would appoint, acceptable for sacrifice. Not, however, until the reign of David, the king

Deuteronomy 12:5-14

after His own heart, did He reveal His chosen place of sacrifice.

THE KING MAKES CHOICES
(II Samuel 24:1-14)

Appropriately enough, the site was revealed on a day when the king himself desperately needed to offer an acceptable sacrifice. Leisure and success had once more begun to take their toll on the sharp edge of his spiritual discernment. In chapter twenty-one, a famine and disaffection among the Gibeonites had been righted, with the result that the prophesied end of Saul's house had at last been fulfilled. In chapter twenty-three, the remaining pockets of Philistine opposition were dealt with. The nation was strong and prosperous, and had gained the respect of its neighbors.

Perhaps because inactivity had made him restless, David decided to determine the military power of the nation by taking a census. God had told Abraham that his descendants were to be without number (Genesis 13:16; 15:5; 22:17). He had told the people through Moses that He was their defense, and their security would be irretrievably tied to their obedience (Deuteronomy 28:1-14; 31:3-8). David himself knew this, as is attested in many of his psalms, including the beautiful Psalm of the Rock which was likely written during his latter years as he contemplated his life in retrospect and saw the Lord's hand through it all.

Pride, and desire for a military display equal to that of the surrounding nations, seems to have clouded David's understanding at this point. Even Joab, old warrior that he was and ever

The events of the last four chapters of II Samuel are not dated, and are obviously not in a chronological sequence. They are added at the end of the book as further evidence of David's desire to serve the Lord.

II Samuel 22

Or, perhaps he was so successful that he was beginning to feel self-sufficient.

prompt to serve his king, was dismayed at the task given to him (II Samuel 24:3). He remonstrated in vain; David was determined to go through with his decision. It may be that his old resentment over Joab's high-handed ways flared up and hardened him in a determination to show who was boss (verse 4).

I Chronicles 21:6

Joab and his aides dallied as much as they dared (verses 5-9) and even then, according to the account of the Chronicler, managed not to finish the job. Nearly ten months passed before Joab reported back to the king, during which time David showed no evidence of rescinding his order, and stifled any warnings of conscience that may have attacked him. Not until the work was finished did David heed the stabbings at his heart and cry out his confession to God (verse 10).

I Samuel 22:5

Through the mouth of Gad, who had been with him as a prophet since his days of hiding from Saul, the Lord gave the repentant king a choice of three chastisements. No matter which he accepted, the work of the census would be undone, for havoc would be wrought among the inhabitants of the land.

David, now once more in fellowship with his God, shows where his confidence truly lies. He would not become the prey of men, but trust himself and his people to the One who had never yet failed to prove Himself merciful (verse 14).

THE KING WORSHIPS
(II Samuel 24:15-25)

The pestilence struck with devastating suddenness that same morning, racing swift as thought through the length of the kingdom "from Dan even to Beer-sheba (verse 15). Jerusalem was the last to be touched, but as the angel of death prepared to enter the capital city, God suddenly called a halt. And the obedient messenger stopped with his sword already drawn against the city (verse 16).

According to age-old tradition, the spot over which the angel halted that day was the very spot where the founder of the nation was stopped with a raised knife in his hand ready to make his beloved son Isaac an offering to God. This had been approximately a thousand years earlier. Now it was the property of one of the defeated Jebusites who, with his sons, was busily threshing grain until the sight of the avenging angel frightened them into running for cover.

I Chronicles 21:20. Many commentators believe Araunah (or Ornan) was the defeated Jebusite king.

David saw the angel, too, and did not know that the God who read his heart had already said, "It is enough." He cried out, not for a mitigation of the judgment, but that he might bear the judgment and his people be spared. David still retained the heart of a shepherd (verse 17). In this, too, he is an illustration of the Good Shepherd about whom he prophesied.

Psalm 23

From I Chronicles 21:16,29,30 we understand that David was already on his way to Gibeon, accompanied by his leading men, all dressed in sackcloth as an outward evidence of their humility and repentance, when he saw the angel and could go no further.

This was as the Lord wanted. He would accept the sacrifice offered from the contrite heart of His under-shepherd, but the manner and place of it would be as He would choose. So, on the spot that was once Moriah and hallowed by the obedience of Abraham, David—as representative of his people—paid for and offered the sacrifice that purchased their redemption from the awful pestilence (II Samuel 24:21-24). Again we see in him a picture of what Christ has done for us.

David understood that this was to be the site God had chosen where He would accept the sacrifices of His people. In the days remaining to him, he made every preparation possible for the long-dreamed-of Temple he was not permitted to build, and instructed his son Solomon in the plans for it. For a thousand years God's people would present their sacrifices on that spot until the day came of which Christ prophesied, "when the true worshippers shall worship the Father in spirit and in truth" (John 4:23). That would be when He Himself became the one necessary sacrifice offered on an altar called Calvary. Have you been to that altar?

I Chronicles 22:1

Today the Dome of the Rock (a mosque) is believed to cover the site of Solomon's temple over which Zerubbabel rebuilt the second temple (enlarged by Herod) which was destroyed by the Roman Titus in A.D. 70.

THE KING'S LAST TESTIMONY
(II Samuel 22:1—23:7)

Had David been a man after God's own heart because of his outward perfection, we would all have cause for despair. He failed God often—no less than did Saul whom the Lord rejected. No, David's greatness was the result of his heart attitude toward the God he called his Saviour (see II Samuel 22:3). David gave glory to God for all that was right in his life and reign; and for all that was wrong he humbly confessed personal responsibility and sought forgiveness. He knew that his throne was a stewardship from God for which he was answerable (II Samuel 23:2). He was a living illustration of the truth of I Samuel 2:30, which we have seen to be the theme of the book: "Them that honour me I will honour, and they that despise me shall be lightly esteemed." More than that, he was a foreshadowing of the Son God promised to him. This Son would fulfill all God's will and rule from his throne forever.

You should have seen Christ as you have studied these two Old Testament books—both in His earthly life, humiliation and death, and in His future exaltation and glory. David, "the sweet psalmist of Israel" (II Samuel 23:1), not only prefigured Him, he wrote of Him. When Jesus said, "Search the scriptures," He was referring to the Old Testament. And the reason for His command was, "they are they which testify of me" (John 5:39).

DISCUSS IT AT HOME

• Of all your activities and achievements, what will seem of most value when you think of the memories you will leave behind?

• Of what special value has this study been to you? What have you learned that applies to your understanding of Scripture? Your personal Christian life? How have you seen Christ in I and II Samuel?

FOOD FOR THOUGHT

"Were God's faithfulness no more unchanging toward us than ours toward Him, what would become of us all?"

—F. W. Krummacher

This is a review test. Match the columns.

(   )   1. The theme of Samuel is

(   )   2. Saul showed his chief aim was to

(   )   3. David's chief aim was to

(   )   4. We see in David's life

(   )   5. God called David

(   )   6. David honored God by

(   )   7. God honored David with

(   )   8. God chose as the place for His name

(   )   9. The site of the altar and temple

(   ) 10. David's summary of a king's duty

a) a man after His own heart

b) Araunah's threshing floor

c) a picture of Christ

d) building the temple

e) David's capital, Jerusalem

f) establish a kingdom

g) faith, repentance, obedience

h) glorify God

i) glorify self

j) he that ruleth over men must be just

k) the Davidic Covenant

l) them that honour Me I will honour

What We Believe

Accent Bible Curriculum adheres to the following statement of faith, assuring you of materials you can use with confidence.

- The Trinity of God
- Verbal, Plenary Inspiration of Scripture
- Total Depravity of Natural Man
- The Virgin Birth of Jesus Christ
- His Blood Atonement
- His Bodily Resurrection
- Personal and Imminent Return of Christ
- Person and Work of the Holy Spirit
- Eternal Security of the Believer
- The Separation of Church and State
- The Autonomy of the Local Church
- Worldwide Missions—the Obligation of Every Church
- A Regenerated Church Membership
- Personality of Satan
- Justification by Faith
- The Reality of Heaven and Hell
- The Priesthood of the Believer
- Two Ordinances Only: Baptism by Immersion and the Lord's Supper